SANTOS

IN MEMORY OF
ALICE BEMIS TAYLOR

FOUNDER OF THE TAYLOR MUSEUM AND

THE COLORADO SPRINGS FINE ARTS CENTER

THROUGH WHOSE INTEREST AND GENEROSITY

THE PRESENT COLLECTION OF

SPANISH AMERICAN FOLK ART WAS MADE POSSIBLE

SAN

THE RELIGIOUS FOLK

THE TAYLOR MUSEUM

TOS

ERT OF NEW MEXICO

Text and photographs by
MITCHELL A. WILDER with
EDGAR BREITENBACH

With a foreword by
Rudolph A. Gerken, Archbishop of Santa Fe

of The Colorado Springs Fine Arts Center

FOREWORD

This book should be received with genuine interest by the American public. In the past few decades, America has begun to realize that Spanish culture has left a most precious heritage of art to our country.

Many Americans travel to Europe and foreign lands to admire the religious art found in great abundance in other countries. Unfortunately, America has been so preoccupied with other development during colonial days and later, that little time was given to an art distinctly American. Spanish colonies in the present Southwest, dating back some 300 years, brought to this country a people essentially interested in spreading the light of the Gospel among the pagans. The Church encouraged the natural inclination of the people to give expression of their religious convictions and fervor in devotions and the arts. It is true that much of the religious art in New Mexico is of a rather crude nature contrasted to European art of the same period, and for centuries the art of New Mexico was not sufficiently appreciated, even by the Church, as a most important contribution to the culture developed in America.

This book is another very valuable contribution to the literature published on the culture in the Southwest of the United States.

Artists of America and Europe have placed great importance upon the very rich culture found in New Mexico and upon the abundant material for those creative people who have learned how to appreciate the Spanish Americans. Fortunately, much material has been collected in recent years representative of the works of both artists and writers of colonial times. These materials comprise the oldest record of Church, State and society existing in the United States. The recorders spoke from the fullness of their hearts in these many beautiful and unusual devotions, both in art and in the written word.

I venture to predict that this book will be received with a warm welcome by a large group of admirers who have already learned something of New Mexican art and history.

RUDOLPH A. GERKEN, *Archbishop of Santa Fe*

CONTENTS

ILLUSTRATIONS

INTRODUCTION

Santo (plural *santos*) is a generic term, used in New Mexico to denote representations of saints or holy persons. When used to designate any specific character, the word becomes a title, as in *Santo Domingo*. The term is used in this book in reference to any representation of the saints or holy persons. A crucifix, a religious print, or a statue are each referred to as a *santo*.

Two types of santos in art are recognized. The statue, or figure in the round, is a *bulto*. The painted board, relief panel, or print is a *retablo*. We have retained the Spanish terminology inasmuch as popular usage throughout the Southwest has gained acceptance for these words in both written and spoken English.

The native religious folk art has been a subject of great interest to residents and visitors in New Mexico for many years. During the past twenty-five years many individuals have collected examples of the craft, finding in them much of the spirit and charm with which the Spanish American is so richly endowed. Today there are hundreds of examples scattered from one end of the United States to the other, testifying to the American love of hunting curios.

The Taylor Museum collection is the result of the interest and generosity of many individuals. The nucleus of the collection was formed through the acquisition of the santos of the late Frank Applegate, of Santa Fe. Mr. Applegate was among the first to recognize the religious art of the Spanish Americans as one of the most vital expressions of colonial culture in New Mexico, and his extensive collection was the result of many years' devotion to the subject.

With the opening of the Colorado Springs Fine Arts Center in 1936, Alice Bemis Taylor presented the Applegate collection to the Fine Arts Center, to be housed and shown in that department known as The Taylor Museum. As one of the most valued features of the Museum, the collection has been enlarged extensively during the past seven years. The present publication is the first to treat of the Taylor Museum materials.

We have frequently been asked, "How do you collect santos?" In this question there is sometimes an intonation suggesting that subtle methods have been used. The images of the saints are, in many cases, Church property, and their public sale, over the counter of a curio store, raises the question of whether the article is not actually stolen property. We can only state that reputable dealers have handled the sale of santos in good faith, and with the full knowledge of local Church authorities.

[13]

The collecting activities of the Taylor Museum have been extensive, and the present collection reflects the generous assistance of many friends of the Museum. Without their cooperation, guidance, and advice the examples illustrated in this volume could never have been assembled. For eight years we have bothered collectors and dealers with requests for photographs and information on santos in their possession. Many of these friends will find their unacknowledged contributions in the text or plates of this volume.

The present work in no way exhausts the subject of New Mexican religious folk art. By force of circumstances this publication is almost entirely limited to the collection of the Taylor Museum, a compromise which could not be avoided. We have been guided in our work by the need for a catalogue of the outstanding examples of the craft which are being shown in a traveling exhibition of Spanish American religious art. Scant attention is paid the retablos; the subject has been consciously avoided inasmuch as William S. Stallings, Jr., of the Taylor Museum, has in preparation a manuscript devoted to this phase of the craft. Unfortunately, Dr. Stallings' paper will not be published until after the present war. The valuable information which he has gathered on retablos has not been used in treating of the ten examples illustrated in this book.

To His Excellency, The Archbishop of Santa Fe, the late Rudolph A. Gerken, the writer is especially indebted. On numerous occasions Archbishop Gerken gave freely of his time in extending interviews and writing letters, and without these contacts, this volume would be sadly deficient. And to the many parish priests of New Mexico, I owe a debt of gratitude. Their patience in searching out information and informants is exemplary of their service in the Southwest.

To other collectors, and in this category I would certainly place the dealers (for they are, in reality, collectors with a sincere appreciation for the materials), my apologies for failure to include in this book many admittedly superior examples of santos. However, as explained above, this work is essentially a catalogue of the materials in a given exhibition, and does not profess to include all the known examples. For the interested reader, the following list covers the major collections in the hands of individuals and institutions.

°Mr. John Kenneth Byard
Norwalk, Connecticut

Mr. John Gaw Meem
Santa Fe, New Mexico

Mr. Gilberto Espinosa
Albuquerque, New Mexico

Mrs. Cornelia G. Thompson
Nambé, New Mexico

Mrs. Meredith Hare
New York, New York

Mr. Cady Wells
Santa Fe, New Mexico

Miss Mary C. Wheelwright
Alcalde, New Mexico

The Brooklyn Museum
Brooklyn, New York

Cathedral Museum
Santa Fe, New Mexico

The Denver Art Museum
Denver, Colorado
[Collected by Miss Anne Evans]

The Harwood Foundation
[University of New Mexico]
Taos, New Mexico

Museum of New Mexico
Santa Fe, New Mexico
[Collection of the New Mexico
    Historical Society]

University of New Mexico
Albuquerque, New Mexico
[Collected by Mrs. Neil B. Field]

*Mr. Bruce Cooper
The Spanish Chest
Santa Fe, New Mexico

*The Fred Harvey Company
Santa Fe and Albuquerque, New Mexico

*Mr. James MacMillan
Spanish and Indian Trading Company
Santa Fe, New Mexico

*Mr. Ralph Meyers
Taos, New Mexico

*The late Mr. James L. Seligman
Old Santa Fe Trading Post
Santa Fe, New Mexico

*Mr. George Travis
Travis Curio Company
Taos, New Mexico

*Collection no longer intact.

There are undoubtedly many collections omitted in the above list. The authors will appreciate any information on other materials which may be known to the reader.

Lastly, a word of thanks to Mr. Harry H. Garnett of Colorado Springs. Without his keen enthusiasm and understanding of New Mexico and the Spanish American people, many of the examples in this volume would be unknown to us today.

To Arnold Blanch go my sincere thanks for inspiration to undertake this work. Through his efforts, the Taylor Museum collection is being shown in eastern centers where the art of the Spanish American has heretofore been relatively unknown. Dr. and Mrs. W. S. Stallings, Jr., must share in whatever credit accrues from the study of santos. Thanks to their interest I was introduced to the religious art of the Southwest.

Francis Borgia Steck, O. F. M., of the Catholic University of America, has kindly read the section dealing with the Penitent Brothers. His welcome suggestions are incorporated in the text. Mr. Weldon Kees, Director of the Bibliographical Center for Research, Denver, Colorado, has given unsparingly of his time in locating source materials. The book has been designed and supervised by Oscar Ogg, whose generous assistance has proved invaluable.

To my patient collaborator and to the Museum secretary, Olive Bradley—many thanks.

MITCHELL A. WILDER

Colorado Springs, March 1943

[15]

SANTOS... THE RELIGIOUS FOLK ART OF NEW MEXICO

THE HISTORICAL BACKGROUND

New Mexico is a broad table of land, tilted slightly to one side in such a way that the northern areas are high, while the southern portion slopes off gradually to the grazing lands of southwest Texas. The table is far from being flat, however, despite the casual impression that the horizon is the only obstruction to our view. Barren mesas cut sharp square patterns into the landscape, evidence of the former surface in the geologic past. In the north, the southern spurs of the Colorado Rockies attain an altitude above timber line. Such variation in terrain, while not immediately apparent, has had a great bearing upon the development of New Mexico's people.

From the southernmost portions of the state to the Colorado line, we pass through several life zones, or areas in which the native vegetation is sharply defined, one from the other, by varying climate. The climatic changes are in turn regulated by altitude. Thus, within a relatively short distance, we may travel from the cotton ranchos of the lower Rio Grande to the tundra wastes of Truchas Peak. In between lies the soft temperate belt which has become the mecca for traveling Americans, and which was selected four centuries ago by the first Spaniard as a comfortable spot for a winter camp.

However, the greatest factor in this land of contrasts is the presence, or absence, of water. The annual rainfall of the area is approximately fourteen inches; not enough for the farmer to eke out a crop before the end of a too short growing season. The only answer to this problem is irrigation, and the greatest source of water is the Rio Grande. This river, rising in southern Colorado, cuts a wide weaving channel across the barren land, marked today by the green of field crops and orchards. It is in this valley, within "ditch distance" of the river, that culture has flourished throughout the centuries.

Before the Spaniards, New Mexico belonged to the Pueblo Indians, who about A.D. 800 took over the land then occupied by a still more primitive group, the Basket-Makers. The new tenants brought with them a knowledge of agriculture which they applied successfully to the difficult conditions of marginal farming along the drainages. Their history is carefully and completely written in the archaeology of the American Southwest. Starting in small wattle houses or pits, their architecture developed to the enormous communal house of several stories, as exemplified by Pueblo Bonito, or the present structures at Taos. Social organization was strongly developed along matrilineal lines, and religious concepts grew into amazingly complex rituals, with a dominant theme of fertility, the continual prayer of the farmer. Material culture was equally rich, with advanced forms in both pottery and textiles. In fact, Pueblo fame spread beyond the geographical confines of the people, for rumors of this cultural bonanza drifted south to Mexico. Such tales falling on Spanish ears were sweet for those who had arrived too late to attend the looting of the Aztec empire. Coronado was off with an expedition by 1540, in search of the golden treasure of Cíbola. In the mind of the Conquistador, organized primitive society and monetary wealth had become synonomous.

The looting of New Mexico was a dismal affair. Cities of Gold turned out to be mud houses in the evening sun. The soft climes of Mexico stiffened to rigorous winter at higher elevations. Insidious "non-cooperation" on the part of Indians put a strain on friendly relations. The Spanish were sadder but wiser, and New Mexico fell into general disrepute.

In the Spanish philosophy of conquest, however, defeat was not to be considered. There were many ways of winning a people, and if financial considerations made military efforts too costly, the Church could always be relied upon for active work in converting the Indians to a Christian concept of life. This task fell to the Franciscan Fathers, who moved into the New Mexico frontier in company with the military, and it was their zealous fate to remain behind after the main body of soldiers had departed.

The real value of New Mexico was never again mistaken by the Spanish. While worthless financially, the colony was maintained as the northern frontier of Spanish holdings in the New World, and in this capacity civil authority, as symbolized by a governor and garrison, were established in the early years of the seventeenth century. The work of converting the native population, as conducted by the Franciscans, was tremendously successful, and the opportunities presented in this field alone were sufficiently attractive to induce the Spanish Crown to hold New Mexico. The Catholic Kings were obligated to do all in their power to spread Christianity in the New World, and the heathen population of the Rio Grande region served as a moral obligation to hold the Spaniards in the country. New Mexico was as much a religious colony as though it had been planned as one.

No frontier is worth holding unless it is fortified by something more stable and binding than the armory full of soldiers. Colonists were needed; people rooted in Spanish ways and beliefs; farmers capable of supplying the growing capital with the everyday needs of life. Therefore, colonials of Mexico were encouraged with generous grants of land to those willing to venture out to the frontier. These grants were quite naturally made in the choice agricultural areas of the Rio Grande valley. Though small, they were excellent, and the colonist understood this type of farming, for it was similar to his own farm in Mexico. Crops were also similar, though restricted to a shorter season. Corn, beans and chile became the backbone of Spanish residence in New Mexico.

In the midst of this peaceful conquest came the rude interruption of Indian rebellion in 1680. For a few years the Pueblos held the Spaniards at a respectful distance; to be exact, near the present city of El Paso, Texas. However, the force of arms again set up Spanish authority in Santa Fe, and people settled down to a century and a half of quiet politics, not to be interrupted until the then embryonic United States asserted her rights in the middle of the nineteenth century.

From 1692, when De Vargas reconquered New Mexico, until General Kearny raised the American flag in Santa Fe in 1846, New Mexico played the part of a "step-child" colony, first under Spain and later as a Mexican territory. During these years politicians and clerics wrestled with one another in efforts to impress the Crown with their "successes" in New Mexico. Diverse opinions of Church supporters, and administrators bent upon asserting the rights of civil authority, frequently split colonial administration. Through it all the humble colonial, removed from the intrigues of the capital, struggled to maintain life, pay his taxes, and find some joy in living.

The one cultural force in this frontier society was the Catholic Church. Education was conducted under its auspices; social activities revolved around Church functions, and the chief communal task for the small villages was the construction, repair of, and contribution to the parish church. As in Old Mexico, life began and ended with the blessing of the padre, and it was only proper that this eminent man should be the guide during the years between. Thanks to his efforts, art found its way into the humble household of the Spanish colonist.

Every adobe house must have a patron saint. This practice is so deeply ingrained in the Mexican way of life that we may accept it as fact. But, in early times the supply of santos, like other items of religious furniture, was severely curtailed. Trade with Old Mexico was carried on under the most difficult conditions. Oxcart trains made slow progress over the *camino real* from central Mexico, and such commodities as were transported over this route were articles of prime necessity for the colony. The demand for religious furnishing grew in direct proportion to the increasing population, and articles manufactured in Spain or Old Mexico were completely out of the question for the average man. The padres found the solution.

The Franciscan Fathers were well trained for their tasks in frontier life. When it became necessary to adapt their traditional architectural forms to a new building material, they evolved the adobe mission style, frequently building the church with their own hands. To supply furnishings for the structure, they were again forced to rely upon their own talents. As men of learning, their role in frontier life placed them in a position of cultural as well as spiritual leaders. Among their number there were unquestionably friars of some modest artistic ability. To these men was assigned the task of creating representations of the saints. Working with native materials, they portrayed Biblical characters in sculpture and painting, in the Spanish tradition.

The need soon outgrew the productive capacities of the friendly fathers, however. The friars offered instruction and guidance to the laity in the manufacture of religious furniture. In a short time the craft of making santos developed into a legitimate business as well as a devotional practice, among the common people.

Two types of santeros (makers of santos) should be recognized, the professional and the amateur. The one created a religious figure as a marketable product. The other worked for more idealistic reasons: the desire to express his faith in and devotion to his religion. To judge from the profusion of examples which have survived, the craft was once tremendously popular.

The professional santero was in the same position as the New England itinerant portrait painter. Both were commercial artists, peddling their products, or accepting commissions for special types of work. The santo maker of New Mexico undoubtedly traveled from one small village to another, accompanied by a burro load of saintly images, selling or trading his merchandise for the produce of the villagers. In the sense that such a craftsman was a full time worker in this specific trade, he probably possessed greater ability as a sculptor or painter than did the amateur who made a santo on less frequent occasions. The better craftsmen developed distinct styles in their trade. Through these individual traits we are able to distinguish the work of one man from that of another. However, in no case was a statue signed by the artist. Our identification of individuals must rest with a description of their personal interpretation of the saints. There are occasional examples of painted boards, retablos, where the artist saw fit to inscribe his name. However, the list of known santeros is so small as to be negligible. The individual is lost in the years, and lives only in his artistic creations.

The religious folk art of New Mexico was created out of necessity, and as it grew, it became the major artistic expression of generations of colonials. Other arts and crafts flourished and prospered in the Southwest, but none received the devotion and care which santos merited, if for no other reason than that they were holy objects. The other crafts were frequently employed to enhance the appearance of a saint. Tin niches, crowns, or sconces might be prepared for the new figure. Carved wood stands might support the image, and the finest of needlework would be offered in form of clothing. As in Europe, the arts found their focus in the Church.

Chronology in this religious art is virtually impossible to establish. By the informal conduct and wide participation in the craft, there was no general development of style, each man finding his own way. In New Mexico the apparent sequence is from the complex to the simplified. The more sophisticated and technically superior examples correspond to the early period when the clergy participated in the work. Gradually the freedom of individual expression brought simplification of forms and the inevitable stylization of the elements. The process grew along innumerable lines of interpretation, the most dominant ones being expressed in the work of professional santeros who created great numbers of santos. Occasionally there is a reversion to European prototypes. In such cases we may assume that it is the work of a padre, or other individual with a formal education. These examples must be considered sophisticated interlopers in an otherwise pure atmosphere of popular art.

Santos are no longer made. Just when the craft met its demise we are unable to say, for it was of such humble state that no one noted its passing. Several factors bear on the sudden collapse of this religious art. After the American occupation, events in New Mexico moved rapidly toward the greater development of the territory. Trade with the east was encouraged, and people were gradually drawn out of their self-sufficient ways. Further, in 1854 a company of French priests was sent to the diocese upon the request of Archbishop Lamy. It is natural to assume that the new fathers found little appeal in the simple folk art of a people who were of another cultural background. Nothing was done to encourage the local artistic tradition, as evidenced by the erection of the Santa Fe cathedral in a style completely divorced from its surroundings. The native arts gradually gave way to the tide of commercial articles. The presence of gaudy plaster statues of saints in the churches today attests to the changing ways of the Spanish American.

TECHNOLOGY OF THE SANTOS

The technique of the New Mexican santero in carving a bulto is so extremely elementary that lengthy description is unnecessary. With very few exceptions, the figure is carved in cottonwood, a light soft wood found throughout the area. This material was a poor choice from the standpoint of the wood-carver equipped with adequate steel tools, for cottonwood is rough, pithy, and splinters readily. However, with the limited resources of the New Mexican, it suited the requirements. The soft material was easily cut with a small knife, and reentrant angles could be worked out slowly without the use of chisels and gouges of various shapes. This is the only possible explanation for the use of an inferior material where an abundant supply of better wood (pine) was available.

The artists never became conscious of or interested in the adaptation of materials to their work. Had there been a feeling for the beauty of wood, as we appreciate it in other sculptured works, sooner or later the native craftsman would have been inevitably attracted to the possibilities of juniper, often mistakenly referred to as cedar. In recent times the novelty carvings executed by José Lopez and his family at Córdova took advantage of the beautiful color and grain of this wood. However, the old santero adhered rigidly to the tradition of gesso and paint over the wood surface, and being essentially unreceptive to innovations for reasons of his conservatism, he left the many possible avenues for the development of native religious art wholly unexplored. Further, there was the tradition of Spanish painted sculpture serving to influence his work, and the unquestionable preference of the people for realism in their saints. This latter factor, probably more than any of the foregoing suggestions, dictated the use of paint over wood (estofado technique).

To simplify the difficulties of carving, as well as to overcome the disadvantages of poor material, the bulto was made in several pieces and later assembled. There are very rare examples in which the work has been carved *en bloc,* and these pieces are of small size, generally less than eight inches tall. With the methods and materials of the New Mexican worker, large pieces of wood were unmanageable. The trunk of the figure, or the entire body and legs, were cut from a single block, depending

[24]

upon the treatment of the legs. If the legs were to be revealed, they were cut individually and attached. Arms and head received the same treatment, and in many cases where the figure reached sizeable proportions, each element of the limb was joined with wooden pegs. Thus, hand, forearm, and upper arm would all be made separately. This method offered further advantages in that greater realism, through variety of gesture, could be introduced in the posture of the figure through the assembling of the various parts.

Nails were never used in putting the figure together. All articulation of non-movable joints was accomplished through small dowels and glue. The figure was then smoothed with rasp and scraper and the surface prepared for the native *yeso* (gesso).

The exact method used in the preparation of gesso is evidently lost to present generations of Spanish Americans living in the region. Inasmuch as santos are no longer made by the people, there is no demand for gesso for the special purpose of preparing a surface to be painted. The following recipe for preparation of yeso for plastering walls, however, is indicative of the process which was probably used. I am indebted to Señora Simon Atencio of Punta de Agua, New Mexico, for this information. Señora Atencio stated that this mixture was the same that was used for preparing wall plaster when she was a little girl. I should estimate her age (1937) as approximately 60 years.

"Mix a gruel of flour and water. One can (approximately one quart) of flour to a
   bucket of water. Cook tierra blanca (gypsum) in oven until white; then grind
   to fine powder. Place this in water and boil until stiff (paste consistency).
   When ready to apply, add the gruel."

The above is a free translation of instructions given during a hilarious conversation among Señora Atencio, her husband, and several curious onlookers. As the labor of mixing plaster and repairing the walls is traditionally a woman's work in Spanish American society, it was considered a special occasion, not without humor, that a male Anglo should request this information.

The quantities used in mixing the ingredients were ill defined, as the correct amount is known through long practice.

The type of gesso produced by this recipe is much too friable to be of service on a retablo or bulto. However, with the substitution of animal glue, either skin or bone type, for flour, the result is comparable to the hard brittle surface which we find on many of the better santos from New Mexico. Such animal glue was readily available and it is safe to assume that it was used in preparing the gesso ground. In some examples the gesso has a slight ivory to buff color, the result of too intense heat during cooking of the glue.

It does not hold from the above statements, that all New Mexican santos were executed on carefully prepared gesso grounds. Not infrequently the entire surface of a retablo has fallen off due to poorly prepared gesso. There is as wide variation in the care exercised in preparing the ground as there is in the artistic merit of the finished product.

The gesso was applied to a retablo in one or more layers. Those examples having thin gesso coats are generally in a better state of preservation than others on which the surface was built up to considerable thickness. The surface of the gesso was either casually smoothed over with a stick, before the mixture was dry, or allowed to dry first and later smoothed with pumice or other abrasive.

Gesso was used extensively in building up specific features of a statue, such as the beard. Frequently a beard might be left out entirely from the carved wooden body of the figure, and later added by modeling in gesso. The ground served an additional purpose in smoothing out the defects of the poor material used in the body. Slivers and cracks, not to mention errors in carving, could be easily disguised under the gypsum coat.

One relatively uncommon technique employing the use of gesso as a modeling medium is shown on Plate 58. By building up the most important features of the picture in plaster, a relief panel was achieved. While never a very popular form of devotional art in New Mexico, relief panels are characteristic of the Spanish American craftsman.

A technique in the construction of a bulto involving the use of cloth and gesso, is far more common. Many figures were carved without legs. The truncated body was supported by a roughly conical framework of light sticks fastened to the base board, and fastened at the top around the waist. The figure was thus held by the radiating framework, over which a cloth, previously dipped in fresh gesso, was tightly wrapped. The cloth shrinks upon drying and draws the frame tight to the body of the figure, insuring adequate support. In this way the artist simplified the task of carving the figure, and overcame the obvious difficulty of weight in carving, in solid wood, the large flared skirt of the Virgin (Plates 4 and 47). A smaller example of the use of gesso on cloth is shown in the Cristo (Plate 36), and while the technique would seem to be better adapted to large figures, there are examples of very small bultos fashioned in this way. (María Santísima, south transept altar, Santa Cruz Church, Santa Cruz, New Mexico.)

The representation of drapery or folds in garments always puzzled the New Mexican craftsman. His sculptural talents were seldom capable of a satisfactory rendering of these elements in terms of the baroque models from which he sometimes worked. The use of cloth dipped in gesso, draped over the figure in the desired manner, achieved the reality which was the delight of all Mexican church artisans, both in the Southwest and in Old Mexico. Cloth prepared in this way was a perfect surface for painting.

Many large figures were articulated to allow movement of the arms. In one example, the Santo Entierro (Plates 26 and 27), additional flexibility was achieved through articulation of the knees, neck, and jaw. The purpose of this elaborate bit of "puppetry" is discussed in the description accompanying the plates. Generally the need for flexibility existed only in shoulders and elbows.

In reenacting the scenes of the Passion, the figure of Christ might be moved through various postures. The erect figure could represent the Ecce Homo, Christ after the Flagellation, the Cross-Bearing Christ, or the Man of Sorrows, dependent upon the position of his hands, and the use of clothing. In the illustration of the Jesús Nazareno (Plate 34), Christ is depicted in the attitude of the Ecce Homo, with hands tied. In this posture the figure might properly be clothed. With little change, the representation might denote Christ after the Flagellation (Christ at the Column). The left shoulder of the figure has been drilled to accommodate a wooden pin, by means of which a cross might be fastened to the shoulder. The arm could then be raised to hold the cross, achieving a new conception of the Saviour, the Cross-Bearing Christ, a popular devotional image in the Southwest and Mexico. Finally, the concept of the Man of Sorrows may be interpreted by the figure with the hands untied and the wounds displayed.

The articulation of these figures in their flexible joints is done very simply and crudely with pieces of leather or cloth. It is generally found on figures which are connected in some way with the Penitent Brothers, though it is not confined to this class of bulto. The need for such manipulation of the figure as described above exists particularly in the type of service conducted by that society, and would be of little importance in the usual devotional exercises.

Of paints and pigments used on the santos we know very little. Even among the Spanish American people of today, and especially those who have taken an interest in the revival of religious art, there is apparently a total lack of knowledge on this most important point. José Lopez, of Córdova, probably the best known of all the recent craftsmen, developed his style without the use of paints. However, another revivalist, Celso Gallegos, of Agua Fría, attempted to paint his bultos. We have no information on the kinds of pigments used, but certainly his results were a far cry from the traditional santos.

In the absence of positive scientific analysis of paint samples, we feel that Gilberto Espinosa's statements on this point should be accepted. (New Mexico Santos. *New Mexico Magazine,* March 1935.) Mr. Espinosa has long been one of the leaders in the movement to preserve the Spanish American cultural heritage in New Mexico. He has stated that earth and vegetable colors of local origin were used for yellow and red. Blue was undoubtedly available in the form of indigo, widely used by both the Spanish American and Indian peoples in their weaving. While this dye is successful in textile fibres where a mordant may be used to hold the color, it is a poor pigment for painting, as the color is unstable. Blue is frequently faded, and where an intense blue does exist, it is generally the result of later over-painting.

The use of gold leaf, gilt, or metallic paints of any variety was unknown in New Mexico in the early period of the santeros' craft. Not only was it economically impossible for the people to afford such materials, but they were unavailable. In later years, gilt was sometimes used in the restoration of figures. The large bulto of San Miguel (Plate 28), displays the use of metallic paints, while the San Francisco (Plate 5), has received a haphazard dash of gilt paint on the top of the head. However, where such pigments are used on the original coat, it is a general index to Mexican origin, though there may be exceptions.

The surfaces of retablos were frequently coated with a poor quality varnish, probably derived from pine rosin. As is inevitable with the use of such low-grade varnish, the surface will become cracked and may darken considerably. The result is, however, not harmful when occurring on a New Mexican retablo. Many of the finest panels exhibit a crackled surface of home-made rosin varnish. It is often possible to reveal a retablo in its pristine state merely by removing the coat of native varnish which has darkened to a deep brown through the years (Plate 56—after cleaning).

Other methods of finishing the surface of a retablo should be mentioned. The use of egg-white as a final over-all coating is known. Mr. Espinosa reports a high lustre finish achieved by use of a polishing stone, or glass knob, similar to the method employed by the Southwestern Indians in burnishing pottery. A makeshift wax surface was sometimes achieved by rubbing the board with a bit of grease, "to bring out the color." The figures in the round were commonly finished with a coat of varnish, glue water, or egg-white, or left with nothing at all over the painted surface.

Repainting a santo was common practice among the people. The obvious need for making repairs to a damaged bulto was the most frequent motive for repainting, while other pieces were repainted with a desire for renovation and "dressing up" of the figure. Many of the bultos illustrated in this volume have been stripped of one or more coats of paint, revealing the original surface. Sometimes this coat is in excellent condition, suggesting that the repainting was inspired rather by the fancy of the owner than for any real need. In refurbishing a saint, no effort was made to employ the colors or pigments used in the original. Any materials at hand, and these were generally of the commercial house paint variety, were used. The result is the obliteration of a great deal of the original character, and in one instance, at least, the complete alteration of the identity of the saint. A badly damaged San Antonio was given a beard, and the tonsure and Franciscan cord painted out to produce a makeshift representation of San José.

The miscellaneous details needed to complete a figure were made through the ingenious use of such native materials as were at hand. Glass eyes, common in Europe and Mexico, were not only unavailable to the New Mexican craftsman, but were beyond his economic means. In their place the santero used plates of mica which could be found in the mountains. Tiny teeth were carved of wood. Wigs of human hair were commonly used, serving the dual purpose of enhancing the naturalistic qualities of the figure, and as a devotional offering on the part of the person contributing the wig.

Mention has been made elsewhere in this book of distinctive style groups which we ascribe to individuals, or groups of individuals. Inasmuch as all santeros worked in a common environment, drawing their inspiration, and their patronage, from practically the same source, it becomes unreasonable to ascribe the development of such styles to outside influences. Rather are they the result of individual abilities acquired through plodding and laborious efforts to interpret sculptured forms. Once a mastery of a given problem has been achieved, the artist employed this knack of execution in all his work. The total of these interpretive mannerisms as revealed in a santo may be termed a style.

Several styles are represented in the accompanying illustrations. As it has thus far been impossible to identify the artists by name, styles have been referred to their apparent geographic centers or to some feature characteristic of the type. Only those styles specifically referred to in this text appear in the following summary.

SANTA CRUZ VALLEY (Plates 12 and 13)

There are figures similar to the above examples in several churches in the Santa Cruz valley. The style is characterized by great delicacy of carving and painting, especially in the face and hands. A long pointed nose, flattened on the ridge, puckered lips, slightly protruding eyeball, and frequently a graceful bend in the torso of the figure are all mannerisms of the artist. Plates 38 and 48 illustrate a slight variation of this style, noted in the fullness under the chin—a double chin. Painting of the dress of the Virgin (Plate 38) is similar to santos on the altar of San Antonio Church, Córdova, New Mexico (upper Santa Cruz valley). For other illustrations of bultos in this group see Plates 2, 10, and 54.

THE "FLAT FIGURES" (Plates 8 and 9)

One of the most commonly encountered styles in New Mexican bultos. The distribution of this type is difficult to determine, examples having been found in many areas. A great many specimens are reputedly from Mora County, New Mexico, and it is possible that the name Mora may be properly applied to the style. The dominant characteristic of this type is the flat body, and the severe impelling countenance. All the features of the face are executed in bold angular forms: the triangular nose, deep arch of the brow, and thrusting chin. Hands are carved in a highly simplified manner, appearing as little combs. Red and black, with blue and yellow trim, are generally used on the costume of the figure. Male figures show square black beards.

On Plate 8 may be seen another feature peculiar to the creator of the "flat figures." With the sculptured elements of the bulto confined to the head and hands, he has treated the body as a two-dimensional plane, to be painted rather than treated as sculpture. The outlining of the figure, to be seen from the frontal view, is the santero's solution to the lack of three-dimensional feeling.

Taos (Plate 34)

This group might be sub-divided to distinguish those examples known to be of Penitente origin, though stylistic criteria must be overlooked if such distinction is to be made. The figures are frequently very large, with articulated arms and extensive use of cloth dipped in gesso (cf. p. 26), mica eyes, and sculptured gesso beards. (Plates 4, 18, 24 to 27, 34 to 37, 42 and 47.)

Arroyo Hondo (Plate 5)

Named for the group of three bultos from the Medina Chapel, Arroyo Hondo, New Mexico. The artist characterizes his work by numerous mannerisms: the full painted beard, extremely long sharp-ridged nose, slightly open mouth, and the heavy bulk of the lower body.

Many stylistic groups will undoubtedly be recognized as more examples come to light. However, it is always difficult to localize such a group unless the santos are found *in situ*.

In the retablos there are frequent examples of direct copying, and often the artist attempted originality of expression, even though he sometimes went beyond his capabilities. Many santeros achieved great proficiency with the brush, using a rapid and easy drawing technique by which we can today identify their work. The Veronica retablo in the Denver Art Museum (Plate 63), is an excellent example of the naive, but skilled, draftsmanship characteristic of the best santeros.

Examples are known wherein there is not only stylistic evidence of copying from a prototype, but actual marks of the tracing are left on the panel. This unimaginative method of making a retablo sometimes produces interesting results. The contour of the figure betrays the source of the model, while the secondary details, such as face and hands, are indicative of the meagre talents of the maker. Such examples are frequently found during the later years of the craft, after 1850.

It is especially interesting to note the influence of prints and engravings as seen in retablos. There was evidently a brisk trade in religious prints throughout the Southwest during the nineteenth century. Prints of Mexican and European origin are common, and, later, Messrs. Currier and Ives sold great numbers of prints, all relating to religious subjects. That such prints served as models cannot be doubted. Even today the cheap "chromo" or calendar top is standard reference for the Spanish American interested in a pictorial representation of the saints.

The art of the santero finds both its inception and its development in the limitations imposed by environment. The craft arose as the answer to the need of a people —a need which would, under other circumstances, have been provided by the usual channels of trade. The very factor which prohibited such trade, the remote position of New Mexico from other Spanish centers, controlled the growth of the arts, forcing the people to draw upon their own experiences for inspiration and expression. The greatest curb upon the development of religious art in this region was the lack of materials and outside contacts. These restraints were blessings in disguise. Had the situation in New Mexico changed at any time during the seventeenth or early eighteenth centuries, we might have expected a northern extension of the arts of Mexico, and the santeros and their work might be relegated to the tremendous total of mediocre provincial work. New Mexican folk art was saved by the very factors which prevented its development in the channels of the European tradition.

THE DEVOTION

The most common act of devotion on the part of the Spanish American people, other than prayer, is an offering of some sort to the saint. Frequently, this offering is tendered in the form of a new garment for the bulto. Many santos possess remarkably large wardrobes, the gifts of devout folk who have expressed their faith in this manner. La Conquistadora, the beautiful bulto of the Virgin brought to New Mexico by De Vargas at the time of the Reconquest, 1692, and by tradition the same which is now on the transept altar of the cathedral of Santa Fe, has a wardrobe carefully ministered by ladies of the parish. This custom, common throughout the Spanish world, was brought to New Mexico in colonial days. It is not uncommon to find a bulto with three or more dresses, one on top of the other, and burdened with small offerings of beads, religious medals, or paper flowers. These tender acts of devotion are a constant reminder of the intimate role which santos played in the lives of New Mexicans.

Not all practices derive from general church usage. There are many purely local devotional exercises carried on within the group immediately affected by such belief. For example, the village of Chimayo possesses a bulto of the Santo Niño de Atocha. By tradition, the Niño is the protector of the fields, and in order to acquaint himself better with the needs of his children, he makes nocturnal excursions through the surrounding farmlands. The result of such wanderings is a very natural wear and tear on foot-gear. The villagers have long made it standard practice to offer the Niño a tiny pair of boots. Such charming tales of the comings and goings of saints in New Mexico have established an interesting religious folklore, some original, but much of it adapted from sacred history and legend to the needs of the country side.

In a land where the necessities of life engulfed all thought of the nonessential, it was natural that legends and attributes of the saints should follow extremely practical lines. The Spanish American found his emotional welfare to be part and parcel of the Church, and all the everyday problems of life, which in the average well regulated society are cared for in the normal process of social relations, were referred to his spiritual experience. The hierarchy of saints might be appealed to in

[32]

even the most trivial cases, as for instance when articles have been mislaid. San Antonio is said to assist in relieving such annoyances. However, if the saint failed to reveal the lost article, it was perfectly proper for the appellant to turn the figure of the saint to the wall, as a reprimand for failure. The most severe measure to be taken against the saint might be the removal of the Niño from his arm. It would be pleasant to conjecture that the many figures of the Christ child missing from bultos are the result of this all too human desire to reprimand people—even saints in Heaven.

In New Mexican religious art, images of the Franciscan saints are always dressed in blue garments. Through association we have generally accepted the brown habit as the distinguishing feature of the Franciscan Order, and this variant in the Southwest has caused confusion in studying the santos. Through the assistance of Francis Borgia Steck, O.F.M., of the Catholic University of America, we are able to offer the following explanation for the use of blue habits in New Mexican art.

Certain groups of friars in Mexico adopted blue habits for their singular devotion to the Blessed Virgin, whose distinctive color by tradition is blue. Thus, the Franciscans of Zacatecas wore blue, while Franciscans of the College of San Fernando in Mexico City wore grey. New Mexico was ministered by friars from Zacatecas. In this way there grew up a tradition of Franciscans in blue habits. It was not until 1897 that the universally adopted brown was ordained by papal decree.

San Acacio is always represented with a group of soldiers at the foot of the cross (Plate 1). These small figures are an integral part of the bulto, and the image of this saint alone, without the soldiers, seldom appears in New Mexico. San Acacio is a minor saint in the hagiological dictionaries, and his relatively frequent appearance in New Mexico remains to be explained. It is difficult to find any direct association between the people and the devotion for San Acacio. There is a small community in the middle Rio Grande valley, called San Acacio. In the hope of discovering the prototype for representations of this saint in the village of his name, the local church was visited and several citizens questioned concerning the patron saint of the town. There is no representation of San Acacio in the village, so far as we have been able to discover.

The consistency with which all santeros employed the symbols of this saint would seem to indicate that all worked from the same model. For the present the question of the prototype and its whereabouts must remain unanswered.

As a footnote to the above discussion of the relatively unknown Roman martyr, Acacius, it has been reported, though without verification, that each soldier in the group depicted at the foot of the cross, is given a proper name by the Spanish Americans. The custom of naming even the most minor characters in Bible stories

[33]

is found in religious drama, such as the Miracle Plays. For the sake of clarity it was necessary to identify all characters in the play by name, and such names became fixed in the mind of the spectator. Religious folk plays were known in colonial New Mexico, and it is entirely possible that the origin of the names for the soldiers is to be found in such a dramatic source.

San Acacio has sometimes been confused with representations of the Good Thief. The character of Dismas, the thief who was crucified at the side of Christ, does appear in New Mexico. The images resemble one another, but the representation of Acacio may be distinguished by the accompanying soldiers, weapons, and a drum at the foot of the cross.

San Ysidro, one of the most popular of all saints in New Mexico, by reason of his particular interest in agriculture, is one of the very few saints whose attributes are nearly always complete. He is also the only saint in New Mexico bearing the outward sign of his patronage. It is said that the Lord sent an angel to assist San Ysidro in the ploughing. All Spanish American representations depict this scene, complete with oxen (Plate 53). A charming tale accompanies the local devotion to San Ysidro. As an industrious farmer, he labored unceasingly, even on Sunday. The Lord cautioned Ysidro, threatening first a plague of grasshoppers (which came), and again, torrential rains (which likewise materialized). In desperation, the Lord visited San Ysidro a third time, threatening to give him a bad neighbor. Needless to say, San Ysidro thereafter observed the seventh day.

In New Mexico offerings to the saints in the Church were sadly limited by the economic plight of the people. The limosna box existed, but must have been beyond the means of the average citizen. Even today the Spanish American frequently makes his contribution to the Church in the form of services rendered or goods supplied. In many cases, the labor of hands is far more valuable than monetary contributions.

There are few instances where offerings of great monetary value have been bestowed upon saints. Clothing, small strands of beads, and an occasional religious medal represent the usual gift. An amusing example of a more personalized gift exists in the case of the Santo Entierro (Plates 26 and 27). In cleaning the figure, numerous small bits of candy were found in the mouth.

Proper identification of the santos is sometimes difficult. This is due to faults both of commission and omission, on the part of the maker. An intangible factor in the santos is that the maker was carrying out the work as an act of devotion, and for this reason the result was primarily his personalized conception of the holy person. Secondly, it might correspond to some accepted pattern dictated by a prototype.

Attributes of the saints were frequently difficult for the sculptor to represent. Further, when they were supplied, they were necessarily small and fragile, readily lost or broken. When such losses occurred, the symbol might be replaced with an improper attribute, either through ignorance of the correct one or intentional change in order to bestow a power more pertinent to the need of the individual. In addition there are the inevitable errors of the artist in copying from a prototype. Inasmuch as santos are rarely dedicated by inscription of the name of the saint, the representation without identification was transmitted from one artist to another.

Plate 58, Nuestra Señora de la Luz, illustrates the confusion which may arise through failure to inscribe the representation. This retablo has been elsewhere identified as Nuestra Señora del Perpetuo Socorro (Our Lady of Perpetual Help). (Cf. New Mexico Magazine, May 1935.) However, the similarity between this representation of the Virgin and its several prototypes both in Mexico and New Mexico, establish positive identification. Such misinterpretations, so readily suggested by the subject matter, are seldom so easily rectified. Not all prototypes of the New Mexican santos have been so faithfully followed by the native craftsmen as that of Our Lady of Light.

The various representations of the Blessed Virgin are by far the most popular subjects in New Mexican religious art, both in bulto and retablo. However, exact identification in specific terms is sometimes impossible for the reasons given above. There are numerous representations of the Virgin and the proper name may refer to her acts or her history, attributes, patronage, or to the geographical locality of the image concerned.

The name "Immaculata" may be properly assigned to many figures, while at the same time local terminology will offer something more definite, albeit less accurate from the standpoint of iconography. The bulto illustrated on Plate 48 has been positively identified by a Spanish American as Our Lady, the Queen of Heaven, while every evidence in the figure itself would seem to indicate the representation of Our Lady of Carmel (Carmen). The liberties taken in naming saints account for discrepancies in much of the data, even when they have been collected from Spanish American people.

Santos were sometimes intentionally damaged for purposes of offerings. Thus, an attribute, or a part of the bulto itself, might be broken off and thrown into the fields or burned. There is evidently an association between this act and the pagan belief that the deity can alter nature for the benefit of man, by returning to its natural element. Santos were also charred and burned in spots for the purpose of obtaining holy ash for Ash Wednesday. MacMillan has reported the use of such ash or carbon scraped from a charred spot on a santo, for medicinal purposes. In many examples burned spots appear testifying to some such devotional practice.

Due to lack of documentation, it is difficult to trace the source of the veneration of many saints in New Mexico. Those more commonly encountered are found throughout the Catholic world, and their presence is to be expected. On the other hand, there are many of the most popular members of the hierarchy absent, or almost so, from the New Mexican list. (MacMillan: *Fifteen New Mexico Santos.*) It is interesting to note the appearance, in retablo form, of some relatively unknown characters in Christian art. Here we find Saints Acacius, Alexis, Longinus, and others of equally remote reputation. Their appearance may be attributed to the interests of the individual venerating the saint, either for specific purposes, or through past association. Sometimes, as in the case of San Acacio, the devotion became popular among the people, and many representations will be found. In many instances, however, we know of but one occurrence of the saint in New Mexican religious art.

Popular devotion was restricted to the more generally known list of the hierarchy. A study of the ecclesiastical archives of the Santa Fe diocese may shed more light on this matter, as statements of the priests of the many churches may very well bear upon the execution and presentation of the santos to the Church.

THE PENITENT BROTHERS

Many santos illustrated in this volume are attributed to the Penitent Brothers, Los Hermanos Penitentes. It is unfortunate, in a sense, that such emphasis has been given this material, for numerically speaking, these works are in a decided minority in the over-all picture of New Mexican art. However, the importance of these bultos as works of art, together with their association with the ritual of the Brotherhood gives them a position of unquestioned value in any discussion of New Mexican folk art. There are few positive trends which can be followed through in the religious sculpture of the Southwest. The ecstatic devotion of the members of the Brotherhood produced one of the distinctive forms readily distinguished from other examples.

Unfortunately, this organization has suffered bitterly at the hands of newspaper feature writers. Today the popular conception of the Penitente lies somewhere between the vision of a political cutthroat and that of a religious fanatic. While there is unquestionably a grain of truth behind the many lurid tales recounting the activities of the Brothers, we wish to emphasize that a considerable portion of the present aura of legend surrounding the subject has been created for the headlines. It is not within the province of this work to discuss the function of the Brotherhood beyond its bearing on the religious folk art. Nevertheless, a brief resumé of the subject may be useful in a fuller appreciation of santos.

The society is an offshoot of the Third Order of St. Francis. Originally, the Third (Lay) Order in New Mexico, as elsewhere, was under the direction of the Franciscan Fathers, offering to the laity opportunity for religious study and penitential life according to a special Rule laid down by St. Francis in 1221. The growth of the Order in New Mexico was sponsored by Spanish Franciscans, and conducted in the same manner as elsewhere in the world. Archbishop Salpointe, former Archbishop of the Santa Fe diocese, infers that the cause of change in the regulation of the Penitents came through the secularization of the missions in the early nineteenth century. With the departure of the Spanish Franciscans and the gradual collapse of their missionary work, the conduct of the Third Order ceremonies fell to the members themselves. (Salpointe: *Soldiers of the Cross,* Banning, California 1898.) The Archbishop was undoubtedly correct in stating that the membership became "an anomalous body of simple credulous men. . . ." The Franciscans being no longer in charge, leadership from the ranks of the clergy was missing for many years. However, from the reports of many priests whose work brings them into daily contact with members of the society, the Penitente of today is a devout Catholic, misguided in some remote localities and in some groups, but usually eager to serve his Church in any way possible. Thus, through the agency of the parish priests, at present a certain authority is exercised over the penitential practices. In the past, however, after the departure of the Spanish Franciscans, it became necessary on occasion for the Archbishop of the diocese to denounce certain extreme ordeals, and to prescribe the nature of penance for the members of the group.

The society quarters are housed in a small chapel (morada) generally located apart from other structures. Such chapels are equipped with church furnishings in the Spanish American tradition. Not infrequently a santo which has been transported from the parish church may be seen in the morada. This is done today with the permission of the priest, and testifies to the friendly regulation which the Church exercises over the Penitentes. In other respects, the chapel appears like any small New Mexican church, with the exception of the adjacent rooms which are used for the preparation of the participants in the Lenten and Holy Week services. These rooms are bare, with only a few benches and an occasional retablo or print on the wall. There would seem to be little to indicate the existence of the terrifying ordeals which are attributed to the Brotherhood.

Two aspects of devotional practice have apparently merged in the Holy Week ceremonies of the Brothers. The services offer an opportunity to the faithful to carry out penance through self-inflicted pain. There is, at the same time, a vestige of the theatrical performance of Biblical stories, as recognized in Miracle plays since the Middle Ages. It is readily seen that this fusion of emotion and reenactment could give rise to more and more realistic interpretations as time went on.

Religious life was admittedly one of the great factors in Spanish Colonial society, and the very devout, but unthinking person, could readily be swept into emotional excesses. Such interpretation must be offered in explanation of the many accounts of actual crucifixion which took place in post-colonial times among the Brothers. The act of penance lost its true character, and became desirable *per se.* Needless to say, it is at this point that Church authorities have found it necessary to reaffirm the purpose of penance and the manner in which it may be practiced.

Numerous methods of penance have been mentioned in connection with modern Penitente ceremonies (Salpointe, op. cit.; Lummis: *Land of Poco Tiempo,* N. Y.

1897; Henderson, *Brothers of Light,* New York 1937). Crucifixion was evidently rare. Crosses of enormous size were dragged on the shoulder from the morada to a point designated as Calvary. Lummis reports a penitent who lay for an unbelievable length of time on a bed of cactus. The most common form of self-inflicted penance is, however, lashing of the back with a yucca fibre whip. The lashes are applied to the bare back, resulting in deep lacerations from the shoulder to the waist-line. These wounds may be said to be the hall-mark of the Penitente of olden days, and appears regularly on figures of Christ used in the Penitente processions. As pointed out elsewhere, this is a local variation of the depiction of the wounds of Christ, for the back was the part of His body receiving the least punishment. The Penitente Brothers have reinterpreted the wounds to accord with their own experiences under the lash.

The large figures of Christ, the Ecce Homo or the Man of Sorrows, are constructed in such a manner that they may be carried in procession. A heavy notched base board is attached, presumably that the bulto may be placed on a litter. At other times of the year the image stands on or beside the altar in the morada, usually fully clothed.

All the large figures of Christ referred to above, have been located in the region between the Santa Cruz valley and the Colorado boundary. These images, which are sometimes almost life size, seemingly originated, or have been retained, in the northern part of the area in which the craft of the santero flourished. Inasmuch as documentation does not exist, we are unable to determine the source of the bultos with any accuracy. The Taos area is evidently the center of this particular development. In two examples (Plates 34 and 37), the craftsmanship indicates that both are from the hands of the same santero. There are numerous other examples of this representation of Christ, and in all probability other pieces by this man can be located. Perhaps the vogue for large bultos was established, or developed, through his labors. In any event, the focus of this style is now found in the northern portion of the "santo area"; the same region in which we now find the most active groups of Penitentes. In this region there is a marked tendency towards extremely large figures not only in the Cristos, but also in figures of the saints. (Cf. Plates 42 and 47, both examples from northern New Mexico.)

The image of Christ in the Holy Sepulchre (Plates 26 and 27) is unique in some respects. The maker of this figure focused his efforts upon the creation of a semi-mechanical santo, neglecting the refinements seen in other examples. The careful articulation of the jaw is the only known instance wherein metal was used in the construction of a bulto. Sheet tin was necessary to solve the difficult problem of a movable jaw. Other representations of the Santo Entierro are known, and those which we have had opportunity to examine are of unquestionably finer craftsmanship. (Figures in the church of Santa Cruz, Santa Cruz, New Mexico, and private chapel of Leandro Duran, Talpa, New Mexico.) In these examples there is no elaboration of the articulated joints, while there is careful attention given the sculptured forms.

The Santo Entierro (Christ in the Holy Sepulchre) was the object of deep veneration, and received many offerings from the people. The tiny morsels of candy placed in the mouth of the figure have been mentioned. There are in addition innumerable sachets pinned to the clothing of the figure, several pillows, some filled with flower petals, and an extensive wardrobe. In our plates illustrating this figure the clothes are removed to reveal the bulto.

In terms of the other bultos, the large Penitente figures are unquestionably late. The materials used in their construction, gesso especially, are inferior. Without positive criteria at hand, we would attribute these figures to the period after 1850.

Many stories accompany the figure of Death. This allegorical phantasy has a special appeal to the New Mexican, and representations of Death, seated in a cart, or sometimes alone on a bench, are known in several localities. The figure is properly an appurtenance of the Penitent Brothers, and is normally housed in their chapel. However, like the santos, the figure may be moved from place to place. For example, the specimen illustrated (Plates 30 to 32) was kept in the house of José Lopez, of Córdova, at the time it was acquired. In the village of Trampas, the figure was "stored" in the baptistry of the parish church.

It is related that upon one occasion the arrow drawn by Death was released, killing a bystander. The significance attached to this event—whether the victim was an unbeliever or a martyr to some cause—is not known. By another account, it is considered good fortune to be bumped by the cart while it is being wheeled in the procession to Calvary. (See caption Plate 32.)

It is difficult to winnow fact from fancy in describing the function of the Penitente figures. Numerous observers have been present at the ceremonies, and from their accounts it is clear that a prescribed ritual of conduct is followed. However, variations and innovations occur in any formalized rite conducted by the laity.

The foregoing statements are presented with a view to understanding the purpose of the bultos created by the Brotherhood in terms of the need enforced by the ceremony.

THE ARTISTIC BACKGROUND

On first acquaintance with the religious folk art of New Mexico one is likely to be struck by what might be loosely termed "the medieval spirit." If this impression is analyzed, one will find that it is based on certain outstanding qualities and features, the intensity of religious emotions expressed in simple forms, which are used repetitiously. The single figure is predominant. It is shown in frontal view and with uncomplicated gestures. The palette is limited to few, but strong, colors. Closer examination will reveal, however, that the impression of straightforward simplicity must be modified. There are some figures which display a considerable amount of sophistication (cf. Plates 12 and 13), and even in works which seem to be quite unassuming, features have been included which betray their derivation from a highly developed art. Thus it becomes evident that one is confronted with a folk art of a peculiar character, that is to say, one which is neither so dependent that its prototypes are always clearly recognizable, nor so autonomous as not to create constant associations in the spectator's mind.

We speak of folk art as opposed to the *art of the styles*. The latter expresses almost exclusively the mental attitude of the upper strata of a nation, and it participates therefore in the continuous changes to which these classes are subjected. In this process it follows inherent laws. Every style will pass from an archaic through a classic into a baroque stage, that is to say, from the simple to the intricate. Folk art, on the other hand, is static, or at least nearly so, by comparison with the perpetual movement within the realm of the styles. It is the expression of the peasant and the village craftsman and similar social groups whose ways of life have changed extremely slowly.

This applies fully to New Mexico. Its folk art was produced by a class of small subsistence farmers and craftsmen whose lives remained approximately the same from the time the country was resettled around 1700, until the infiltration of Anglo-American civilization in the nineteenth century. The timelessness of this art makes it impossible to arrive at any chronology on the mere basis of stylistic analysis. There was, it is true, a class of large land owners in New Mexico. Yet they were too few in number to form a cultural standard of their own. Whatever art was created for

[41]

them locally—e.g., the San José of 1783 in the Taylor Museum, which was painted for Don Gaspar Noriega—was a poor version of some model from Mexico or Spain.

Folk art gives form to the creative powers of the community rather than of the individual; common doing and common belief are the soil from which it grows. Folk art has, generally speaking, a strong feeling for the useful. A class which has to struggle for its existence, can afford to embellish an object of its environment only so long as the adornment does not interfere with its proper function. A chest with richly incised ornaments or with painted decoration is more desirable than a plain one, provided it also fulfills its practical purpose as a piece of furniture. Similarly, the fine carving, colorful painting and elaborate clothing of a New Mexican santo is good, not so much because it enhances the beauty of the piece, but as an act of devotion for the Deity or its intermediaries, the saints. Behind such a gesture lies the hope that the saint will graciously return the favor.

This attitude has its bearing on the selection of the subject matter. Although folk art carries along a rich treasure of motifs and symbols of considerable antiquity which date back to a time before the separation into classes had taken place, its new motifs are largely derived from the art of the styles. The choice is usually made with great discrimination. Where it is not a matter of merely selecting ornaments, but of representations, the subject matter is of foremost importance. The reproductions of this book give a fair cross-section of New Mexican art, showing clearly the underlying principle of selection. With the exception of a very few sporadic cases, the religious folk art of New Mexico is completely unnarrative. This is obviously not accidental, but is dictated by an attitude which demands that even a religious representation serve a purpose. The santos are images, by means of which the faithful can communicate directly with a holy person. This immediate contact can, however, be brought about only through a single figure, for any pictorial description of a historical event, whether in sculpture or painting, creates a reality which is distinct from that of the worshipper. In this reality, presented by the picture, the holy persons are preoccupied with their own affairs. The faithful are placed in the role of mere spectators; they can watch them, but can no longer address them.

Saints provide the subject matter for most of the figures and paintings. In a country which was missionized by the Order of Saint Francis, it is not surprising that preference has been given to the Franciscan saints. Yet some of the great Jesuits are venerated as well, in addition to a number of saints who had always been popular. The saints have their definite place in the daily life of the people. The tradition of the Church has assigned patronages to many of them. Thus the faithful can direct their prayers to the saint who has the special power of intercession in a given situation. In our description of the plates, we have tried to identify the patronage of the individual saint on the basis of the European usage. The conclusions at which we arrive by means of analogy seem to be justified in view of the strong Catholic tradition, but do not exclude the possibility of local variations; a saint may have additional powers ascribed to him in a particular community.

Another group of santos is formed by images which are closely connected with the rites of the Penitente Brotherhood: the large Christ figures representing the Man of Sorrows, the Ecce Homo, the Santo Entierro, and the Death Cart. As we have shown in our descriptions, these figures appeal most strongly to the emotions of the Penitentes, who rid themselves of the burdens of sin by reenactment of the Passion of Christ. An image such as that of the Man of Sorrows, whose body is disfigured with bleeding wounds, is their great example, and one which they ardently attempt to follow as far as human endurance will permit.

Related to this group are a number of devotional images. As in Spain, far more emphasis is given to the symbolic meaning of the Crucifixion than to the historical setting of the event. The worshipper does not wish to be distracted by accidental details, but wants to concentrate his devotion, mentally and emotionally, on a single object. Hence the popularity of the images of the Sorrowful Virgin, the Dolorosa, the Soledad Madonna, and of the Christ child, which are completely isolated from any narrative context.

From these images it is but a short step to those which owe their fame to special miraculous powers. Our Lady of Carmel, of Refuge, and of the Rosary, the Camino Madonna and the Virgin of Guadalupe, reflect the devotion for the Mother of Christ.

Religious symbols and allegories play only a minor role in New Mexico. There are, it is true, a number of retablos showing the Heart of Christ, and a few representations of the Holy Cross. On the whole, however, the abstract religious symbol had as little appeal to the New Mexican as the narrative picture. Such complicated subject matter as the Allegory of Redemption on Plate 60 is a rare exception.

As we have already explained, folk art is exposed to a constant stream of influence from the art of the styles. Yet, while this process usually takes place within common regional confines, in New Mexico the nearest source from which inspiration could come was the far away mother country to the south, whose own art was at that time principally derived from Spain.

As in its iconography, the stylistic basis of New Mexican religious folk art is the Spanish Baroque, even though the way in which this influence was exerted is not yet entirely clear to us. With the exception of La Conquistadora in Santa Fe, the San Francisco of the Santa Cruz morada, and a few other isolated examples, no Spanish or Mexican sculpture has been preserved of which we can say with certainty that it was in New Mexico at the time when the bultos were made. Yet many of the figures seem to betray their derivation from some sculptural prototype. We must assume, then, that at least a few statues, which were subsequently lost, were brought over the hazardous roads from the south. Some of the bultos, however, and probably all of the retablos, are derived either from paintings, or more often, from prints. Future research is likely to succeed in tracing more of these prototypes than is possible at the present time.

The Spanish heritage is more strongly in evidence among the bultos than among the retablos. During the Baroque, Spanish sculpture developed definite national features, of which the most striking ones are a strong naturalism and a wide range of psychological expression. In its best creations, this trend in Spanish art produced sublime versions of reality, while its lesser works bordered on the banal. The almost exclusive material for sculpture was wood, which was painted with rich natural colors. Glass for the eyes, and beads for tears, genuine hair and real clothing were used as devices to make the illusion of reality a perfect one. The popular appeal of this kind of sculpture was universal. During the Church processions, especially before Easter and on Corpus Christi Day, the figures were carried through the streets, singly or in groups, and exposed to public worship. At intervals the procession would halt and actors would perform a religious play from an improvised stage. Thus religion formed a bridge between the arts and the people.

In varying degrees all these features can be observed in the New Mexican bultos. To be sure, everything has been reduced to a simple, workable formula. Nearly all the statues stress the frontal view. Whenever the character of a figure permitted, it was given a long and often smoothly sculptured garment, which made unnecessary the representation of legs and feet. Thus many figures have a rather columnar appearance. Counter-post and similar motifs of balance are rarely attempted. Likewise, the gestures are most simple; apart from praying and expressing grief, the hands as a rule do little more than hold an attribute. Yet in spite of all this, the rendering of the faces leaves no doubt that the aim of the wood carver was to approach reality as closely as his ability would allow. Frequently one reads on these faces a distinct psychological expression. Eyes are always strongly emphasized. Eyebrows and lashes are as a rule carefully designed. On larger figures thin mica plates are sometimes placed in the eye-socket, the lips are often open as if in speech so that teeth and tongue become visible, and the skull is covered with a wig of natural hair. Clothing of the figure finally helps to perfect the illusion, however weird and incongruous the result may seem to us.

The popular appeal of this art was perhaps even greater than in Spain, for religion was for the people of New Mexico one of their few emotional outlets. The great

[44]

Church festivals marked the important events of the year in which the whole population took part, whether actively or as pious spectators. Although the processions were less sumptuous than those in the great Spanish centers of Catholicism, their elements were fundamentally the same. They included the display of the larger figures and the dramatic reenactment of religious scenes. Thus all the features peculiar to Spanish baroque sculpture are present in the bultos of New Mexico. Moreover, Spanish and New Mexican sculpture have in common a certain uniformity of appearance, and a prevailing mood of somberness.

The gulf between the art of the styles and folk art is even greater in New Mexican painting than in sculpture. While the sculptor had basically the same aim, that is, the portrayal of reality, the retablo painter did not even bother to preserve a vestige of three-dimensional space in the creation of which the baroque painter had made enormous progress. Instead, he reduced his illusionistic model to a plane, linear pattern. In this process he was helped by the fact that in many instances he copied from prints whose linear scheme made such transformations fairly easy. Complicated overlapping and foreshortening was avoided as much as possible, and wherever it had to be attempted, the result was likely to be a failure. As in sculpture, the frontal view, or at least the three-quarter view, was given preference over any other form of representation. Emphasis was laid on the outlines of figures and objects, which were usually filled in with simple colors. The guiding principle was the clearness of the representation, however short an unskilled painter might have fallen of his goal. To some extent the retablos may have served as substitutes for sculpture, since they could be produced more easily than the bultos. In their best examples, the New Mexican retablos show a strong feeling for pattern and design, as well as for color.

New Mexican religious folk art shares the fate of all other folk art inasmuch as it gradually disappears as soon as industry begins to put cheap machine-made substitutes on the market. This happened in New Mexico after the middle of the nineteenth century to an ever-growing extent. Since the subject matter is of foremost importance, and formal qualities are merely the unwitting result of the creative abilities of the craftsmen, such mass-produced trash is, as a rule, eagerly absorbed. It is true that for some time the works of the craftsman and the new pseudo-art live side by side, as is still the case today. Yet the very fact of their co-existence proves fatal to the older forms, for apart from the subject matter, people with untrained eyes are generally interested in the question of how a thing has been done. Shallow as the modern works may be, in purely technical respects they are often superior to the older ones which, for all their sincerity and unsophisticated beauty, frequently suffer from the limitations imposed by the primitive tools of the santeros. As the result of such comparison, the New Mexicans begin to feel apologetic for their art, and thus the ground is prepared which makes them willing to part with their treasures. At this stage the collector appears on the scene, as happened in New Mexico about 1915. Prices which are low at first, gradually rise and provide a new incentive for sale. Here and there a reaction sets in. Some New Mexican communities are proud of the works of their fathers and cling to their santos with commendable fervor.

With the change of social conditions, New Mexican religious folk art belongs to the past. Recent attempts to revive it were bound to result in failure. Today little more can be achieved than the preservation of the works still extant, to serve as a record of a way of life forever gone.

FIGURE 1. *St. Wilgefortis*. Engraving, mid-18th century, formerly collection of Dr. Voos in Bracht. (G. Schnürer and J. M. Ritz: Sankt Kümmernis und Volto Santo. Düsseldorf, 1934)

FIGURE 2. *Nuestra Señora de Guadalupe*. Original tilma in the shrine of Our Lady of Guadalupe, Mexico.

FIGURE 3. *Virgen del Camino, Patrona de Pamplona*. (Carlos Sarthou Carreres: La Iconografía Mariana en España. Boletín de la Soc. Española de Excursiones. Tomo 37, 1929. opp. p. 112)

FIGURE 4. *Murillo, The Holy Family*. Formerly Munich, Gallery Heinemann. (Works of Murillo; Classics in Art Series, vol. 16)

FIGURE 5. *Volto Santo, Lucca Cathedral*. 7th to 8th century (?). (From G. Schnürer and J. M. Ritz: Sankt Kümmernis und Volto Santo. Düsseldorf, 1934)

[47]

BIBLIOGRAPHY

GENERAL WORKS

Crawford, J. P. Wickersham, Spanish Drama before Lope de Vega. Rev. ed. Philadelphia, 1937

Holweck, F. G., A Biographical Dictionary of the Saints. St. Louis, Mo., 1924

Karlinger, H., Deutsche Volkskunst. Berlin, 1938 (Propylaeen Kunstgeschichte. Suppl. vol.)

Knipping, J. B., De iconografie van de Contra-Reformatie in de Nederlanden. Hilversum, 1939

Künstle, K., Ikonographie der Christlichen Kunst. 2 vols. Freiburg i. B., 1926-1928

Mâle, E., L'art religieux de la fin du Moyen Age en France. 4 ed. Paris, 1931

Mâle, E., L'art religieux après le Concile de Trente. Paris, 1932

Mayer, A. L., Spanische Barock Plastik. München, 1923

Rouanet, L., Colección de Autos, Farsas y Coloquios del siglo XVI. 4 vols. Barcelona, 1901

Solá, Miguel, Historia del Arte hispano-americano. Barcelona, 1935

Spamer, A., Das kleine Andachtsbild vom XIV. bis zum XX. Jahrhundert. München, 1930

Weisbach, W., Die Kunst des Barock. Berlin, 1924 (Propylaeen Kunstgeschichte, vol. XI)

Weisbach, W., Spanish Baroque Art. Cambridge, 1941

Weise, G., Spanische Plastik aus sieben Jahrhunderten. Reutlingen, 1927 et seq.

GENERAL WORKS ON NEW MEXICAN RELIGIOUS ART

Carroll, Charles D., Miguel Aragon, a Great Santero. (El Palacio, vol. L, no. 3, March, 1943)

Espinosa, G., New Mexican Santos. (New Mexico Magazine. March, April, May, 1935)

Espinosa, J. Manuel, The Virgin of the Reconquest of New Mexico. (Mid-America, v. 7, no. 2, N.S.)

Halseth, Odd S., Miscellaneous articles on New Mexican santos in El Palacio, 1928, 1929, 1934

Henderson, A. C., Brothers of Light. New York, 1937

Hispanic Society of New York, Ten Panels Probably Executed by the Indians of New Mexico. 1926

MacMillan, J., Fifteen New Mexican Santos. Santa Fe, 1941

Mangravite, P., Saints and a Death Angel. (Magazine of Art, March, 1940; p. 160-165)

[48]

N. S. de Guadalupe; N. S. de la Soledad

    Carreras, C. Sarthou, La iconografía mariana en España. (Boletín de la Sociedad Española de Excursiones. vol. 37, 1929, p. 60-72; 110-132)

    Tormo, E., La Inmaculada y el arte español. Madrid, 1915

    Vossler, K., Die Poesie der Einsamkeit in Spanien. 1940

El Niño Jesús

    Praz, Mario, Studies in 17th century Imagery. London, 1939 (Studies of the Warburg Institute. vol. 3)

La Santísima Trinidad

    Troescher, G., Die Pitié-de-Nostre-Seigneur. (Wallraf Richartz Jahrbuch. vol. 9, 1936, p. 148-168)

Santa Librada

    Schnürer, G. and G. M. Ritz, Sankt Kümmernis und Volto Santo. Düsseldorf, 1934

Carreta de la Muerte

    Sorrento, L., I "Trionfi" del Petrarca "a lo Divino" e l'allegoria religiosa negli "Autos." (Estudios eruditos in memoriam de Adolfo Bonilla y San Martín. Madrid, 1930, p. 397-435.)

    Weisbach, W., Trionfi. Berlin, 1921

    Whyte, F., The Dance of Death in Spain and Catalonia. Baltimore, 1931

Penitentes

    Fisher, Reginald, Notes on the Relation of the Franciscans to the Penitentes. (El Palacio, vol. XLVIII, no. 12, December, 1941)

    Lummis, Charles F., Land of Poco Tiempo. New York, 1897

    Salpointe, J. B., Soldiers of the Cross. Banning, California, 1898

N. S. de la Luz

    von Wuthenau, A., The Spanish Military Chapels in Santa Fe and the Reredos of Our Lady of Light. (New Mexico Historical Review, July, 1935)

    Walsh, William J., The Apparitions and Shrines of Heaven's Bright Queen. New York, 1904. Vol. 3, p. 239-249.

ILLUSTRATIONS

The saint wears the uniform of the Spanish colonial army of the late 18th c. A bandoleer is hanging from the left shoulder across the breast. Trousers and undergarment are blue, with red ribbons tied around the yellow stockings. The yellow coat is lined with a red material. The red all-over pattern may be interpreted as either an embroidered appliqué, or as slashes; neither of which seems consistent with this particular uniform. However, it may be that this detail which occurs with some persistency on a number of representations of this saint, has been inherited from an earlier prototype.

Red and bluish black colors prevail in the garments of the small assisting figures, which represent soldiers. With one exception, their weapons have been broken off. The drummer on the right seems to have played a special role in the Spanish American version of this scene, for even where no soldier companions of the saint are shown, as happens in some examples, the drum still appears at the foot of the cross as an attribute.

According to the legend, San Acacio was, at the time of the Roman emperor Hadrian, the leader of 10,000 Christian soldiers who suffered martyrdom on Mount Ararat.

The story relates that the Lord gave the 10,000 martyrs at the hour of their death the power of bestowing health and earthly goods upon all who would cherish their memory. For this reason, their leader, Saint Acacius, was included in the group of the Fourteen Helpers in Need, and it is in this very capacity that he might have appealed to the people of New Mexico. San Acacio's popularity is further attested to by the fact that according to an oral tradition the soldiers under the cross have been given names, a custom which perhaps originated from a saint's play.   [*Height of main figure:* 22″; *Height of small figures:* 5¾″]

St. Anthony of Padua with the Christ child is a subject matter which has received such widespread recognition through the paintings of Van Dyck and Murillo, that it is difficult to realize its origin as not older than the High Renaissance and that its great popularity dates only from the Baroque.

Donatello's scenes of the life of St. Anthony in the Santo at Padua do not yet include this group, for the Quattrocento was attracted above all by the many spectacular miracles of the saint. The charming but unassuming legend which tells how St. Anthony was seen one day by his host as he was holding the Christ child in his arm, was discovered only in the age of the Counter Reformation, when mystical contemplation once more turned toward the childhood of Christ, as it had done before in the days of St. Francis. The cult of the Christ child (cf. pl. 33), of St. Joseph (cf. pl. 18), and the popularity of this legend have their common roots in the emotional religious sentiments of the 16th and 17th centuries. Whether St. Anthony or St. Joseph, the image of a virile saint who lovingly holds the Divine Infant, wholly absorbed in this tender play, had an enormous appeal to an age whose feeling vacillated between contrasting principles. It is not surprising that this subject matter had its greatest success in Spain, the center of Catholicism at that time.

The New Mexican bulto has been done with considerable skill. The figure of St. Anthony is lively and of graceful proportions. His face shows youthfulness and refinement, features which are customarily given to him. St. Anthony appears in New Mexico with great frequency.   [*Height:* 14¼″]

"Santa Barbara doncella,
Líbrenos del rayo y la centella."

This little prayer is still spoken in New Mexico, when a thunderstorm approaches; for Santa Barbara is the great protectress against lightning and fire.

She has been given these extraordinary powers on account of an event which followed her martyrdom. It is told that Santa Barbara, daughter of a wealthy heathen in Roman times, was kept by her father in a tower. When he left one day for a long journey, he had a bath house built for her, which was to have two windows. On his return he discovered that his daughter had adopted the Christian faith, and, as an outward sign of her conversion, had changed the number of windows from two to three in honor of the Holy Trinity. In his anger the father brought her before the prefect, who condemned her to death. He even carried out the capital punishment himself, but Santa Barbara had hardly given up her soul when the unbelieving parent was struck down by lightning as the penalty for his cruelty.

During the Middle Ages Santa Barbara was chosen as a patron by members of those professions which either cause explosion, or suffer from it: artillery men and miners. While these functions are of certain importance in New Mexico, she has another great power which concerns every faithful Catholic. A passage in her legend relates that when she had fulfilled her martyrdom, she was granted by God the privilege of intercession on behalf of those who have honored her memory. Because of this, she has become one of the Fourteen Helpers in Need, and together with San Cristóbal she takes care that all who believe in her do not die unprepared.

The attributes of Santa Barbara vary somewhat in New Mexican art, especially in the bultos. There are examples where the symbolism of the windows has been forgotten, as in the present figure. Instead a new symbol has been introduced: the saint wears a three-tiered skirt of different colors, green, yellow, and slate blue in this case. In some retablos this new attribute is the only one by means of which the saint can be identified. The correctness of the interpretation is in one instance attested to by an inscription. The motif of the three-tiered skirt as a Trinitarian symbol is possibly derived from a saint's play.

Henry Swinburne in his *Travels through Spain in 1775 and 1776* relates that a friend of his had seen the year before in San Lucar a play entitled, The Conversion of Santa Barbara. A monk, attempting to prove to him the mystery of the Holy Trinity, formed three pleats with his habit and let them drop again. These three pleats, he explained, which belong to the same piece of cloth, are the image of the three divine persons. (Cf. L. Rouanet, v. IV. p. 226.)

Loaned to the Taylor Museum by Mrs. Meredith Hare, New York, N. Y. [Height: 18″]

The similarities in technique and style between this figure and the Rosary Madonna (pl. 47) are so striking that we may safely ascribe both works to the same craftsman.

In technical respects, they are identical: a carved half-figure has been placed into a wooden frame which has then been covered with painted cloth.

The ornaments on the white skirt consist of pale blue tendrils, which end in ocher colored buds. Both colors are also used for the border of the skirt.

The physical forms are round in both instances; cheeks and chin are puffy, even the hands are fleshy and coarse. Although the Virgin is wearing a white blouse, her shoulders and elbows are tinted red, as it is customarily done in New Mexico in the rendering of the nude body. It may well be, however, that these reddish marks, as well as the painted breasts, are later additions of a fanciful restorer.

The psychological expression is dramatic and lively. Mica plates give the eyeballs a natural glance, and in the half open, sorrowing mouth, the upper row of teeth is visible. The figure lacks the restful qualities of the Soledad Madonna (cf. pl. 12); instead it portrays the Virgin as she weeps under the cross.   [*Height:* 41″]

Plate Five

SAN FRANCISCO DE ASÍS

[Denver Art Museum]

While the iconography of this figure is identical with that of the St. Francis on pl. 6, its style differs considerably.

The coloring is rather unusual. The saint is dressed in a slate blue monastic habit. Dark blue lines have been painted along the folds, on the arms and around the collar. The color of his face is ocher, the hair golden, except for the black hair line. The beard is black. Red is used on the lips and on the nimb, the shape of which originated in Italian renaissance sculpture.

The features have very striking characteristics. The mongoloid eyes have the shape of a crescent. Their outline is repeated on the mouth, the beard, the center part of the hair line, and in the side view of the ear. Cutting through this system of rising lines is the abrupt ridge of the long nose, the shape of which is continued in the pointed triangle of the beard.

The figure is leaning slightly to the left. This treatment, together with the gesture of the balanced arms, cancels the ponderation of the body; the figure seems to be weightless, as if suspended in air.

The Taylor Museum has recently acquired three remarkable santos which are closely related to the one illustrated here. These santos, representing San Francisco, San Buenaventura and San José, come from the private chapel of Juan Medina in Arroyo Hondo, New Mexico, whose family has venerated them for generations. The facial characteristics of all three saints show a strong resemblance to those described, while the figure of St. Francis shares with ours the peculiar motif of balance. [*Height:* 31″]

This figure is possibly associated with the Taos group (cf. pls. 18 and 34 and p. 30). It was executed with a considerable degree of skill; the proportions and the gestures are convincing and the well modeled head is full of inner life. Though the artist's approach is a markedly realistic one, this tendency is kept within proper bounds.

The Franciscans of the Post-Renaissance period envisaged the founder of their order under the aspect of a saint of the Counter-Reformation. St. Francis, the mildest in the hierarchy of saints, whose love for the animated world was all-embracing, was then represented as an ascetic, with hollow cheeks, meditating over a skull upon the vanity of earthly things. It is this trend which our figure reflects. The cranium which St. Francis holds in his hand is the correlate of the introspective mood on his face. Only the cross which he extends with his right arm toward the spectator, establishes a link with the outside world. St. Francis has become a symbol of conversion and penance.   [*Height:* 22½"]

Santa Librada is a martyr venerated in Spain as early as the 12th c. She was beheaded in Aquitania at the order of her own father. Her cult flourished especially in Sigüenza. During the 17th c. the legend of Santa Librada was merged with that of a saint who had never existed, and who was variously called St. Ontkommer, St. Kümmernis, or St. Wilgefortis (virgo fortis).

What gave rise to the cult of this peculiar saint was a crucifix whose fame was unparalleled since the 12th c.: the Volto Santo at Lucca, which shows the bearded Saviour on the Cross dressed in a long tunic (cf. fig. 5). The fascination which this cross exercised upon the faithful was largely due to its unusual appearance. For in the 12th c. people were already accustomed to picture the Crucified Christ as dressed merely in a loin cloth and wearing a short beard. Beyond the Alps copies of the Volto Santo were held in high esteem. While the memory of their connection with the Lucca cross was preserved through the centuries in most cases, in some the tradition was weakened. Unaware of the origin, people called these strange looking images of Christ, St. Helper, since they believed that a Crucifix of this type was endowed with special powers. In one instance, finally, the tradition was completely lost, and as a result the legend of a new saint originated.

This happened in Steenbergen in North Holland, around 1400. People whose prayers had been fulfilled began to inquire into the nature of the image which had brought about such miracles. They thought the crucified person dressed in a long robe represented a woman saint. A legend sprang up which told of a king's daughter who had refused to accept the husband whom her father had found for her because she had secretly chosen Christ. In her anguish she prayed to Him for help, whereupon Christ let a beard grow upon her face. As a result, her suitor withdrew, and in extreme anger, her father had her crucified. Since her real name was unknown, she was referred to as St. Ontkommer, the one who takes away cumber and grief.

The cult of this imaginary saint soon spread to Germany and Northern France. Representations of her from the 15th to the 19th century are very numerous (cf. fig. 1). She proved to be a great helper in distress, and though some scholars recognized the truth at an early date, thanks to popular devotional literature, the cult has continued to exist practically until this day. On the authority of Canisius, the saint was included by Molanus in his edition of Usuard's *Martyrologium* (1568), and from there into the official *Martyrologium Romanum* (1583).

Molanus, a Flemish scholar, had the unfortunate idea of latinizing the name Ontkommer with St. Liberata. Although he dropped this form of the name later, the damage was done. For the Spaniards and Portuguese, greatly flattered that a flourishing cult of their own Santa Librada existed in far away countries, seized upon the opportunity to declare both saints identical. (Cf. *Martyrologium,* Coimbra 1591; *Dexter Chronicle,* Saragossa 1619.)

The merging of two legends which have only a faint similarity was a difficult undertaking. While the miracle of the beard was never fully accepted in the Iberian Peninsula—we know of only very few monuments which show this detail—the crucifixion of St. Ontkommer became permanently part of the new version of Santa Librada's legend. Since the 17th c. the Spanish Librada is represented in this manner. Her cult was brought to the New World and the Republic of Colombia counts her among her patron saints even today.

In stylistic respects the bulto shows all the characteristics of the santero of the "flat figures."

[*Height:* 12½"]

Although this santo has no attributes in its present state, the position of the left arm seems to indicate that she formerly carried a child. On this evidence, we tentatively identify the figure as some concept of the Virgin.

Whoever turns the pages of this book will soon recognize that this dour looking lady bears all the marks of the craftsman who produced the "flat figures." Front and back are perfectly plane. The yellow trimmed black coat forms a frame around the red dress. The pointed chin, the sharp nose, the drawn cheeks, and deep grooves over the eyes, are all well known devices which that unknown santero used in numerous repetitions.   [*Height:* 25½″]

Plate Nine

NUESTRA SEÑORA

[Detail from Plate 8]

We have tentatively identified this bulto as St. Francis Xavier (1506-52), the great Jesuit missionary who preached Christianity in India and in the Far East, because New Mexican representations of this saint show him in a costume similar to the one worn by our figure. Like many of the more recent saints, St. Francis Xavier does not have a specific attribute in art. Instead, he is usually given a crucifix as a general symbol of his pious devotion.

This santo carries a book in his right hand, while a green cross is attached to his head. We are unable to give any valid reason for the peculiar position of the cross, since we do not know of any similar piece. Perhaps it may be the result of a misunderstanding, but it is also possible that the cross was added later, for the green paint stands out distinctly from the black and white color scheme of the figure.

Over a black cassock the saint wears a white surplice, the borders of which are trimmed with blue and white stripes. The figure is built up with architectonic firmness; the columnar basis formed by the black undergarment, is surmounted by the protuding cylindrical form of the white robe. The angularity of the arms and the stiff ends of the stole enhance the impression of balance and stability. At the same time they create movements which lead upward in the direction of the head.

The head is of the same stern monumentality as the body. The features are clear and strong. Conventionalization and realism are kept in an even balance. The bold nose is matched by the firm chin. A black beard frames the mouth, with red lips slightly opened. The eyes are delicately contoured with minute lines which soften the rigidity, while the upward glance introduces a human element. *[Height:* 23"]

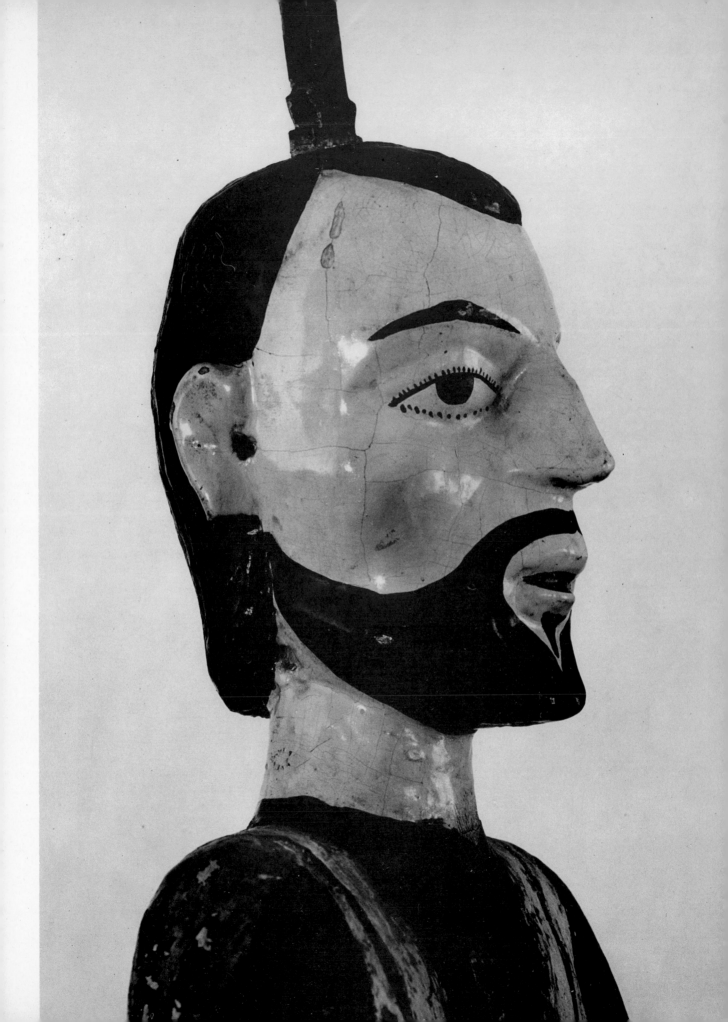

Plate Twelve　　NUESTRA SEÑORA DE LA SOLEDAD

[*Mater Dolorosa*]

The spirit of loneliness and sorrow emanates from this delicate little figure. The lithe body, gracefully bent, is enclosed by a long, black cloak in an unbroken contour. Like a shelter it protects the Virgin from disturbances of the outside world. She is alone with her grief. In her mind she reviews once more the dreadful experiences through which she has just passed. Yet, though her memories revolve around events on earth, her spirit is directed towards Heaven. As if in answer to this inner uplift, the forms within the sheltering cloak are rising, beginning with the arrow shaped folds lightly drawn on the red garment, continuing in the praying hands, culminating in the eyes, tired from tears, yet searching for contact with an invisible realm above, ending in the sharp angle of the hairline. We may see such fine features elsewhere; the Santa Rita (pl. 13) is a sister of this figure. Both are excellent examples of the style which flourished in the Santa Cruz valley.

Our Lady of Solitude is one of the profoundest manifestations of Spanish mysticism during the Golden Age. However, the spirit of loneliness is not confined to this subject alone, but is rather the expression of a mental attitude which pervaded the whole age, and which has left its imprint on Spanish religious art and poetry alike.

The sculptured image of the Soledad was created in 1565 by a student of Michelangelo, Gaspar Becerra. It reached its perfection under the hands of José de Mora and Pedro de Mena. Its popular appeal was very great, for it spread rapidly, not only through Spain and her dominions in innumerable variations, but was also taken up by French and Italian artists.

Considered historically, the type of Our Lady of Solitude has developed from the late medieval Virgin of Sorrows. During the Baroque both types continued to exist side by side. Yet while the older image nearly always included narrative or symbolic elements (the implements of the Passion, seven swords alluding to the Seven Sorrows of Mary), the new type no longer needed such accessories. A century which saw the birth of modern psychology under the leadership of the Jesuits, was prepared to understand its full implications.

[*Height:* 13¼″]

During the Baroque period Spanish sculpture developed typical national features, of which the most striking one is naturalism. Popular religious sentiment required of the sculptor that his saints should appear as lifelike as possible, as though they were actors in the religious plays.

It is to this general trend in Spanish art that Santa Rita belongs. The body is well proportioned, the head neatly cut, and great care is taken in the rendering of eyes, nose, and mouth. By the side of the average expressive, straightforward santo, this saintly lady has an air of sophistication. The delicate little hands which formerly held the attribute, speak so vividly to the spectator that the impression of an actress in miniature is fully realized.

The figure belongs to a group whose members all show these characteristics in varying degrees (cf. the Soledad Madonna on pl. 12). We can locate this style in the Santa Cruz valley.

Santa Rita de Casia (Cascia) is of Italian origin, and lived in the beginning of the 15th c. She was most unhappily married, and after the murder of her husband and the death of her sons, she entered an Augustinian convent where she excelled in ascetic penance. Her attributes are a crucifix and a skull (lost in this instance), and the stigma on the forehead. Her recent canonization is a belated official acknowledgment of a cult which has existed for centuries, especially in Spain and her dominions. There people turn to her as the "Abogada de los imposibles," helper in desperate cases. [*Height:* 16½"]

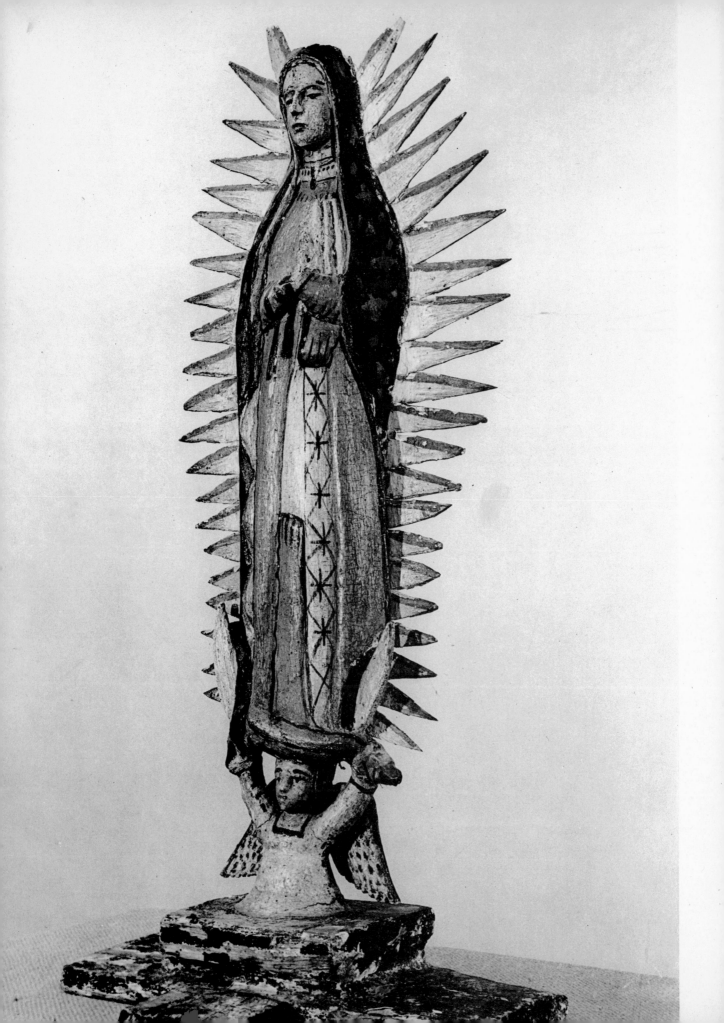

We shall deal with the legend of the Guadalupe Madonna on pl. 62. The centerpiece of the retablo and this bulto are identical in iconographic respect. In both instances a linear and graphic style has been substituted for the painterly treatment of the prototype. The original Guadalupe wears under her cloak a brocaded garment reflecting the light on the left side. This detail has brought about the peculiar color division on the dress of this santo (red and yellow). Of similar origin is the distribution of green and blue on the cloak.

The type of the praying Virgin, standing on the moon and surrounded by a large halo, has grown out of the Medieval illustrations for the Apocalypse. "And there appeared a great wonder in Heaven; a woman clothed with the sun, and the moon under her feet, and upon her head a crown of twelve stars:" (Revel. XII, 1). This Apocalyptic Woman was interpreted as representing the Virgin as she existed before the beginning of time. In the second part of the 15th c. the idea of the Immaculate Conception gained greatly in importance, and as a result the artists tried to invent an appropriate symbol for it. After various attempts, they found it in the Apocalyptic Woman.

We can follow the gradual development of the problem towards its final solution. Around 1500 there originated in French art the picture of the praying Virgin surrounded by the symbols of virginity (e.g. Heures, Thielman Kerver, 1505). While in this example the figure is lacking the sun halo, the latter is present in an engraving of a French 15th c. edition of the Canticles (Mâle, Fin du M. A., p. 213). There the Bride is represented under the image of the Apocalyptic Woman (although the moon is missing). Signorelli's Immaculate Conception, on the other hand, shows the Virgin floating on a cloud and supported by angels, a motif which subsequently played an important role in our theme. At about that time Italian artists, especially Raphael (Sistine Madonna) developed the well known type of the Virgin, though not the Immaculata, standing on a cloud. These are all stepping stones towards a solution which must have been fully reached not long afterwards, for in the Guadalupe Virgin (1531) the type of the Immaculata has already received a definite form. Since the image of Guadalupe became known in the Iberian Peninsula through numerous replicas at an early date, it contributed very strongly to the later development of the Immaculata theme.

The style of the Guadalupe Madonna (cf. fig. 2) displays Renaissance forms at their height. The rigid frontality is eased by a slight turn of the bust and by the bend of the head. The drapery is broadly treated, unburdened by small details. The face has the soft oval shape of the Italian Madonnas. The halo has lost its graphic character.

The 17th century is the Golden Age of the Immaculate Conception in art. The quiet restraint of the Guadalupe Madonna was abandoned in favour of great ecstatic movements, a grandiose élan which affects the whole composition. Whether we take Murillo's or Montañes' Immaculate Conception, or any other, we notice everywhere the intense movement which seizes the whole body of the main figure and forces the simple axial system into complicated curves in manifold directions. The painterly treatment now permits giving a perfect illusion of unlimited space, flowing clouds, and miraculous light phenomena.

In time our Guadalupe bulto follows the baroque creations. Iconographically it is closely related to the original Renaissance image. In style there reappear features which were last seen at the end of the Middle Ages.   [*Height:* 20¾"]

The religious problems connected with this saint have been discussed in our description of pl. 21. While in that instance the great archangel has been changed into a little putto dressed in a light fluttering garment, this example has lost the angelic attributes completely, except for the bright yellow star on his breast and the sign of the cross on his tonsure.

The dress of this figure is unique in New Mexico. It consists of short trousers and a tight-fitting jacket resembling a leather jerkin. The jacket is ornamented with geometrical patterns consisting of triangles and rhombi, which are tinted with red, ocher, and slate blue. The lines on the trousers, on the other hand, are merely incised and without color. We are unable to offer any explanation for this strange costume, except that the pattern may have been suggested by similar motifs used on New Mexican tin work.

There is a strange contrast between the angularity of the surface pattern and the rotund sculptured forms. These begin with the legs, especially the upper thighs, continue in the trunk and the bulging shoulder parts, and culminate in the fascinating shape of the head. The falling half-rounds of the eye balls and brows, and of the hair line correspond to the rising crescents of the chin and lower lip. The concave shape of the cheeks is surmounted by the wide, smooth forehead. As if these curved surfaces were not sufficient, the whole head is bent in the cheek line (cf. pl. 16). This illustration also shows the peculiar form of the ear which is divided into two distinct ellipsoid parts.

The head of the figure shares its striking features with that of one of the Penitente Christs (pl. 52). Since that figure is probably of relatively recent date (ca. mid-19th century), we may assume that this santo was made at about the same time.   [*Height:* 23″]

Plate Sixteen

SAN·RAFAEL

[Detail from Plate 15]

This image of St. Joseph is obviously derived from the same prototype as the magnificent figure of the saint which is described on pl. 18. Both hold the Christ child on one arm, the flower staff in the other hand. Their dress is identical in shape and in color. It consists of a long green shirt and a yellow scarf wrapped over the left shoulder, which is a vestige of the classical costume. Since there is a further striking similarity in the system of the folds, we may be justified in assuming that genetically both figures are close relatives.

In spirit, however, as well as technically, the differences are great. This is the work of a straightforward craftsman of modest abilities. All the devices which gave the other figure a lively character are missing. The folds are arranged symmetrically, no feet are shown, and consequently no problem of balance appears. The head, though neatly cut, lacks the animation which the other statue possesses to an extraordinary degree. Poorest in execution is the child, more a doll than the image of life.

The unfavourable result of the aesthetic comparison does not, of course, affect the religious significance of the bulto. For the man who turned to this San José in his prayer, it may have been no less inspiring than the other artistically better one. [*Height without crown:* 20½"]

The medieval church neglected St. Joseph almost completely, and the artists who followed the instructions of the ecclesiastical authorities, represented him merely as a side figure in scenes of the Christ child and of the Virgin. Wherever he appears, it is as an aged, bald man who humbly assists, rather than acts on his own initiative.

The splendid rise of St. Joseph's cult began, when in the days of Luther the church was in need of new heroes. The Dominican preacher Isolanus gave the signal. His book "Summa de donis s. Josephi," published in Pavia in 1522, was received by the clergy as a startling revelation. The monks of Mount Carmel assumed the leadership in the new cult, followed by Franciscans and Jesuits. The great Carmelite saint, Santa Teresa, placed twelve of her monastic foundations under St. Joseph's patronage and over the entrance to her convent in Ávila (Spain), one of the earliest statues of the rediscovered saint can still be seen.

The Militant Church demanded strong and forceful fighters, on earth as well as in Heaven. To fulfill this requirement, St. Joseph had to be rejuvenated. A dispute arose concerning his age, and in the end most theologians conceded that the saint must have been in his prime at the time of his marriage to the Virgin. Only a strong man, it was said, could have given her proper care and protection.

As a result the artists developed a new type. Instead of a bald man, bent under the burden of the years, they gave him features of youthfulness and strength. Innumerable sculptures and paintings portray him in this way, either alone or, more often, with the Christ child on his arm. It was this latter type, filled with human tenderness, which appealed strongly to the nuns. While in the age of St. Francis the relationship of the Mother and Child was the object of meditation, one now contemplated the emotions of the foster father.

The bulto does not convey such lyrical sentiments. On the contrary, it is singularly force-ful and virile. Legs apart, the saint stands firm and erect. The rendering of the slender body lacks the usual monotony of axial symmetry; the middle fold of the skirt is moved over to the right, the bust bends slightly towards the left, and the direction of the head finally restores the balance. The scarf which is wrapped around his left shoulder completely encloses the space between upper arm and body, a device which is rather unusual in New Mexico. Most remark-able is the facial expression, the penetrating glance of the mica eyes, the raised eye brows, and the open mouth with its row of teeth. Both Joseph and the Child address the worshipper. Instead of tenderly caressing His foster father, as so many paintings depict Him, He has turned towards the world with the gesture of blessing. Curiously enough, He gives this blessing with His left hand.

St. Joseph, the only patriarch of the Old Law in the world of the New, carries as his attri-bute a staff decorated with flowers. It is a symbol of virginity. On the strength of this virtue, the saint has the power to protect those who have recourse to him, from earthly temptation. While this function has played an important role in his cult in Europe, it may not have done so in the stern world of New Mexico. His popularity there is more likely to have been due to another power bestowed on him. St. Joseph, who died the happiest of deaths in the presence of Christ and the Virgin, can secure for the faithful an easy transition from this world to the next. He is the "refugium agonizantium," he who helps man in the hour of agony.

[*Height:* 31½"]

Plate Nineteen

SAN JOSÉ

[Detail from Plate 18]

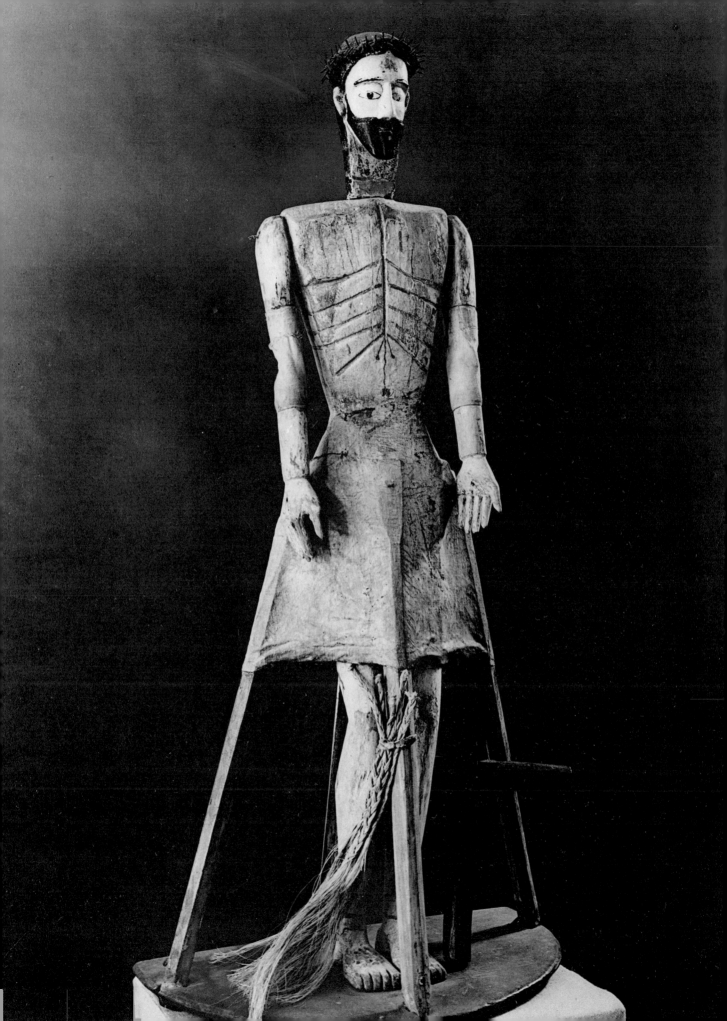

Plate Twenty **CRISTO**

In contrast to the Man of Sorrows on pls. 36 and 52, this figure shows the more usual type; the nude Christ as he appeared on the Cross. From the hips down the figure is enclosed by four braces in order to assure its stability. A piece of blue painted muslin holds the four sticks together and provides the figure with a short skirt.

The treatment of abdomen, breast, and neck, which are perfectly plane, as well as the rendering of the head with the deep grooves over the eyes, shows the stable characteristics of the santero of the "flat figures."

The whip of the flagellation and the cross are symbols alluding to the Passion of Christ. They are also the main implements used during the Easter ritual of the Penitentes.

[*Height:* 38½"]

The style of this figure differs from that of most of the santos. Instead of the usual simplified rendering of the garment, which avoids complicated folds as much as possible, layers of gesso have been applied to the body of the figure and worked into a system of irregular folds. As a result the little statue is filled with the gay and happy spirit of the Rococo, a rather unusual feature in the stern world of the New Mexican saints.

The deliberate change in style was not dictated so much by artistic considerations as by the subject matter. The Book of Tobias tells us that it was St. Raphael, the archangel, who, in the guise of a mortal, protected young Tobias on the long journey he undertook in order to secure the miraculous fish which was to heal the blindness of his father. This story is the basis for the firm and general belief that Raphael is the protector of the traveller, especially the youthful one. In fifteenth century Florence few sons of the great merchant families were sent abroad without the protective image of St. Raphael leading Tobias by the hand. It is therefore not surprising that in New Mexico, where distances were great and dangers numerous, the people prayed to this saint for assistance.

As in other instances, New Mexican art transforms the story into a symbol. No longer is Tobias shown, but only the saint with the fish, which becomes his attribute (lost on our figure). In this process San Rafael himself adopts the boyish features of Tobias, and as a result the powerful archangel of the Old Testament is changed into a putto.

San Rafael having been turned into a little angel, his garment had to be changed accordingly. It had to be airy and fluttery, suitable for the celestial home of its wearer. Only the bare knees and the long stockings which are part of the traveller's dress, still remind us of the costume in which the Renaissance artists used to represent him.

This rejuvenation is a baroque feature which affects many subject matters. Thus, the aged St. Joseph becomes a man in the prime of his life (cf. pl. 18); Murillo's numerous Inmaculadas are young girls, while his angels are infants, and the cult of the Christ child becomes one of the most popular devotions of the 17th and 18th centuries (cf. pl. 33). [*Height:* 18"]

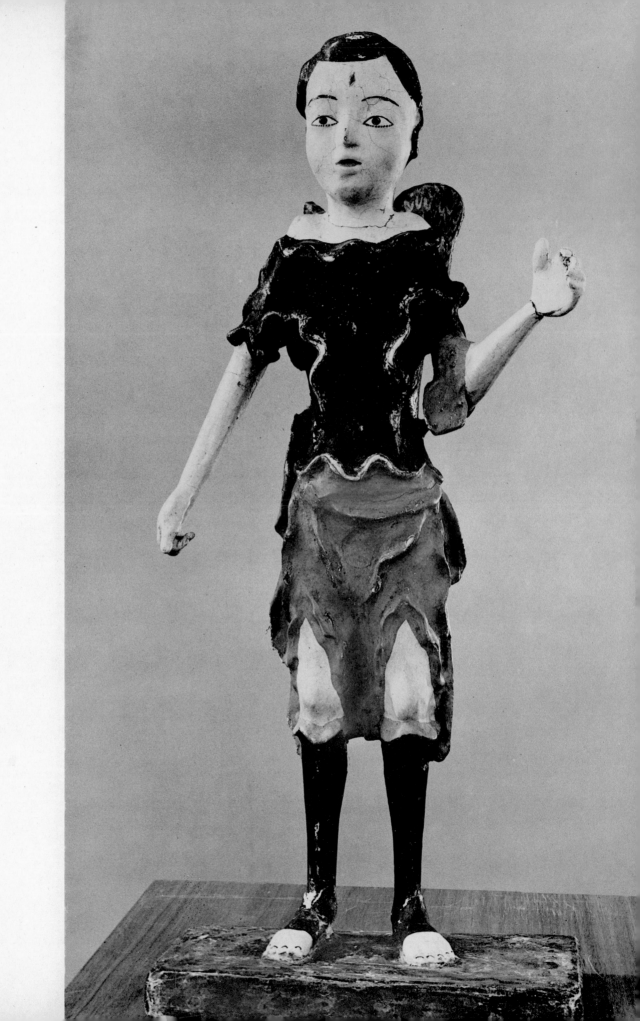

The cult of the Precursor of Christ goes back to the early days of Christendom. During the Middle Ages he became one of the favourite saints of the Franciscan friars, for a man who had lived the life of an ascetic and ardently preached repentence, was obviously dear to the Mendicants, and especially to the Third Order of St. Francis, the Order of Penance.

St. John the Baptist is usually represented with a lamb in accordance with his words: "Behold the Lamb of God which taketh away the sins of the world." (John 1:29). Since the late Middle Ages John the Baptist sometimes appears in northern art in the scene of the Crucifixion, where he replaces the centurion as a witness for Christ. On the Isenheim altar, Grünewald has represented him in this way, standing under the cross and pointing up towards the Saviour. The explanatory inscription is taken from St. John's gospel (3:30), "He must increase, but I must decrease."

This, therefore, is the origin of the type to which our New Mexican santo belongs, a St. John pointing upwards. However, owing to the figure having been detached from its context, the meaning of the gesture has changed accordingly. Our St. John no longer points toward the crucified Christ, but towards Heaven; that is to say, he is represented under a new aspect, as the great warner against the perils of the Last Judgment, when he will sit at the side of Christ. Implicit in this warning is an exhortation to do penance as long as there is yet time.

The striking feature of this figure is its unusual, almost aggressive force. The saint strides toward the worshipper, who is held enthralled by the glare of the eyes, the domineering forehead, and the imperative gesture of the raised arm. On closer analysis, we notice that the striding motif, which first appeared on late medieval German figures of the saint, is scarcely more than indicated. Moreover, the folds of the garment are merely hinted at by incised lines, and were it not for our knowledge of the Biblical story we could not realize that the brown parts of the otherwise white dress are vestiges of the camel-hair cloth which St. John was accustomed to wear. If this figure is so convincing, it is because its style keeps a happy balance between the perceptional elements which appeal to the eye and the conceptional symbols which we grasp with our mind. [*Height:* 26½"]

The attempt at realism is very apparent in the head of this crucified Christ. If seen from a distance, the eyes appear to be closed; yet the narrow slit through which a last glance escapes, indicates the presence of life. His lips are open; a row of teeth is visible in the mouth. The beard is soiled with streams of blood. Human hair on the head and the unusually naturalistic rendering of the beard enhance the illusion of reality.

In the anatomy of the body abstract forms are blended with natural ones. The muscles on the upper arm and the breast protude plastically, but the ribs are merely indicated by incised grooves, and the knee caps have the form of large discs. Congealed blood surrounds the opening of the side wound. In this deep hole a wick has been inserted, which presumably during the Easter rituals was soaked with red liquid which slowly dropped out of the wound. It was collected into a chalice which an angel was holding. The angel is lost now, but the iconographically similar crucifix of pl. 46 gives us an idea of the original arrangement.

[*Height:* 36″]

We have left this figure of the Man of Sorrows in the dress with which it was decorated when it was last serving religious functions in a church. The clothing of sculptured images is a habit which was practiced throughout the Catholic world. Yet while in Europe, outside the Iberian Peninsula, this custom was confined to figures of great popularity, especially those of the pilgrimage shrines, it became a commonplace in the Spanish speaking countries during the Post-Renaissance period.

The dresses, sometimes elaborately made and ornamented with jewelry, are usually offerings, given to the image by pious worshippers in gratitude for special favours or for miracles performed on their behalf. As a result, some famous images possess wardrobes of a very considerable size. Here the inherent Spanish pleasure of imitating reality merged with the desire for making votive offerings. In the churches of New Mexico we can still witness the startling effect of this custom. Many figures are so completely veiled in their garments that it renders difficult any judgment of the artist's original intention.

The life-size Man of Sorrows wears a green robe over a white shirt. Were it not for the wounds on hands and feet, one might be inclined to call the figure an Ecce Homo. We shall discuss on pl. 34 the interrelation and merging of similar pictorial types.

The head is of an extraordinary expressiveness. The natural brown hair which is of the same color as the beard, enhances the realistic side of the work. Yet on closer view, these illusionistic qualities vanish and instead the graphic means of expression become strongly apparent. (Cf. pl. 25.) The curved outline of the beard corresponds to the evenly spaced streams of blood on the wide forehead. Their shape is in turn repeated in the narrow, fine lines of the eye lashes. Beard and mustache form a dark frame around the pale oval of the mouth, while eyebrows, cheekbones and whiskers emphasize in concentric circles the large black eyes. In this way, eyes and mouth, the two centers of psychological expression, stand out strongly in the composition of the face. There are few figures which convey the feeling of utter desolation more strongly than this anonymous work from New Mexico.   [*Height:* 65″]

The Easter ceremonies of the Penitente Brotherhood embrace a number of rituals, one being the reenactment of the Passion. For the last stages of the Passion, following the Crucifixion, a puppet is often times used. As it rests in the coffin, we see it in the last act of the performance. It is, however, fashioned in such a manner that it can be fixed to a cross, taken down, dressed, and laid into the coffin. It is possible that it was even used in some resurrection scene; but this must remain purely conjectural as long as we do not have eyewitness reports of an actual performance.

The legs and arms are pliable at the knees and the shoulder joint, in order to facilitate its fastening to the cross. The side wound is deepened so that a wick could be inserted (cf. pls. 23 and 46). Neck and jaws are movable. There are strings attached to both of them which come out at the back of the head. A participant in the performance could pull the strings and make Christ speak or lift His head, whichever the scene required. Surprisingly enough, the eyes are open and cannot be shut.

The colors of the figure are a reddish yellow for the flesh tints, and red for the blood is freely used, especially on the shoulders and on the back (cf. pl. 34). The ribs are outlined with pale blue, the loin cloth is dark green and gray-brown with narrow red stripes in between. Hair and beard are black.

A figure which has to meet so many technical requirements can hardly reach a high artistic level at the same time. Yet, while its artistic qualities are less than those of the large figures of the Man of Sorrows, it is invaluable as a document of religious folklore.

[*Height of figure:* 68″]

Plate Twenty-seven

EL SANTO ENTIERRO

[*Detail from Plate 26*]

SAN.MIGUEL

St. Michael, the archangel, is among the saints for whom St. Francis had a special devotion. In his great love for mankind he was deeply attracted by a saint who weighed the souls on a scale with mild indulgence and rescued them from the devil in the hour of death. While the cult of St. Michael is widely spread, we always find it in the wake of the Franciscan mission.

It is true, our group does not show St. Michael in this capacity, yet there is one feature which is at least reminiscent of it. In the palm of his open hand the saint holds a loop of the chain with which the devil is fettered. This gesture, which seems to be highly inappropriate at a moment where force is to be applied, can be explained by examining other representations from New Mexico or elsewhere. There we may observe that the saint is holding the scales on a chain exactly as he is holding Satan here.

While the care of souls is St. Michael's perpetual function which will culminate in his participation in the Last Judgment, his greatness has already been proved in the very beginning of time. When Lucifer, led astray by pride, placed himself at the head of the revolting angels, he was overcome by St. Michael and thrown out of Heaven. As he fell, his angelic features changed into devilish ones. This is the scene which is shown by our group. St. Michael has set his foot upon the victim, a Roman gesture of victory, and with his raised sword he is about to finish off his adversary. His gaudy costume in green, red, and yellow is a far cry from the armour which the late medieval artist used to give him. The theatrical aspect also prevails in the winged devil with a satyr's head.

The bulto is reputedly the one which stood on the main altar of the church of San Miguel del Vado.   [*Height of group:* 28"]

Ever since early Christian times Job has been the symbol of faithful reliance on God. St. Gregory the Great's (d. 604) moral explanation of the Book of Job became one of the classics of Christian literature. Since the late Middle Ages, Job's story was presented on the stage of the religious theatre. Throughout the centuries the vicissitudes of his life were depicted in art. When in the course of the Counter-Reformation a need for new devotional images arose, the figure of Job was one of them. Detached from its narrative context, it became an "exemplum patientiae," symbol of Christian patience.

This admirable little bulto shows Job seated in accordance with the Scriptures, though a wooden seat has replaced the dunghill. Except for the loin cloth, his well modeled body is nude. He is completely covered with boils. Job supports his head with his right hand, a gesture of contemplation, while at the same time his left arm is bent horizontally in a rather strained position. The implied active character of this gesture counteracts the passiveness of the other one: Job is engaged in patient meditation, not in inert brooding. Mental activity is likewise reflected from the inward expression of the eyes.

As a patriarch of the Old Testament, Job has been given a place in the hierarchy of the Christian saints. He is a patron against morbus gallicus, syphilis.

The tin niche in which Job patiently contemplates his condition, is made of an old gasoline can. From an account (published in "Tin Crafts in New Mexico," introduction by Carmen G. Espinosa, New Mexico State Department Vocational Education, Santa Fe, 1937), we learn that during the time American troops were quartered in Santa Fe, people bought empty oil cans from the soldiers. The ingenuity of the Spanish American in devising useful objects from the meagre materials at hand often brings about astonishing results!   [*Height:* 14½"]

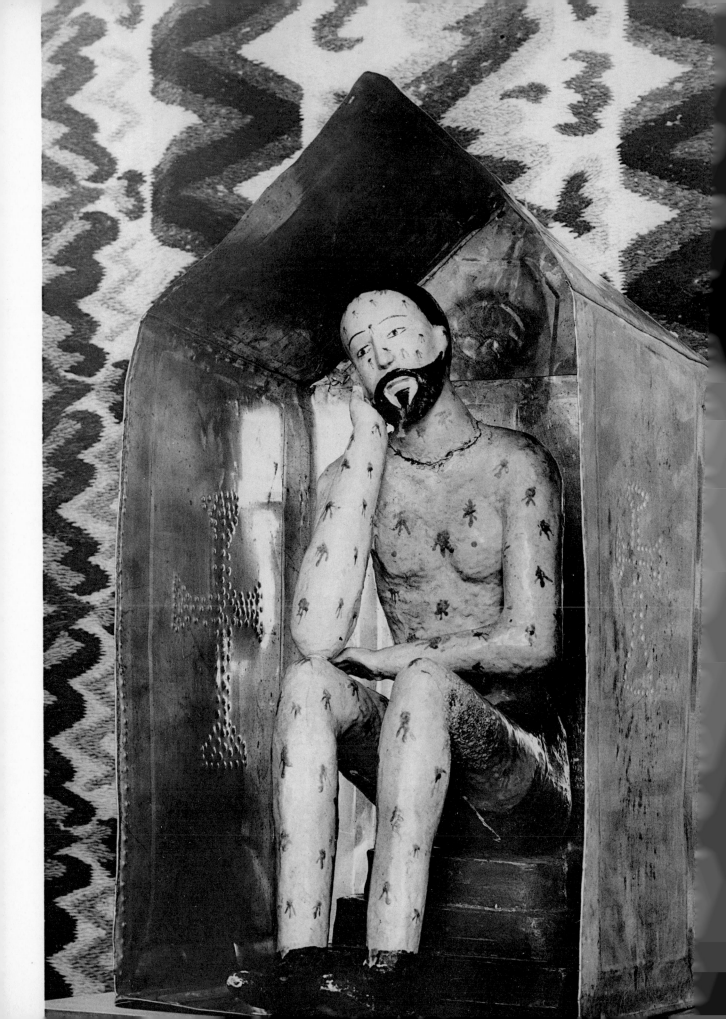

During the nocturnal rites of Holy Week, the Penitente Brothers employ in their procession a cart on which sits the figure of Death. They drag it along among the flagellants and cross bearers. Mrs. A. C. Henderson, who witnessed the rites, has given us a vivid description of it. (Henderson, *Brothers of Light,* 1937, p. 32 seq.) She tells us of the lurid impression of the scene. Death was clothed in a rust black dress with staring obsidian eyes in a chalk white face. Whatever faint light fell upon them was reflected by the black crystals, thus giving the skull a terrifying illusion of life.

The cart which Mrs. Henderson saw was very heavy. Its wheels were stationary. To drag it up hills and around corners with rough ropes slung around the bare shoulders of one of the Brothers, was an act of penance in itself. It is very likely that the idea of penance, which is no longer present in our light and movable cart, was originally an indispensable part of the whole conception. There is, however, one detail in Mrs. Henderson's report which seems to indicate that even her procession had no longer entirely preserved the original meaning. She tells us that the procession took place during the night of Thursday and Friday before Easter. In our description of the Man of Sorrows and of the Santo Entierro (pl. 26), we have pointed out that the idea of reenacting the Passion of Christ forms an integral part of the Easter rites of the Penitente Brotherhoods. Christ died on Friday afternoon and was buried the same day. The hours that follow the entombment until the moment when, on Easter morning, the jubilant news of the Resurrection is received, are the most desolate ones in the whole Church year. It is then, when Christ is in His tomb and during His descent to Hell, that Death triumphs on earth. There can be hardly any doubt that the original idea is that of the Triumph of Death during the darkest moments of the work of the Salvation.

The idea of triumph is of Roman origin. Its aim was the glorification of the victorious general. Originally based on religious beliefs, it gradually became, under the emperors, a symbol of secular fame and honor. Christianity cannot tolerate the glorification, which is reserved for the Deity and the saints, being given to an ordinary human being. As a result, the triumph disappeared at the time when Christianity became the basis for the new post-antique civilization. Throughout the Middle Ages the natural human desire for fame, which could not be suppressed completely, had to find other outlets. With the coming of Humanism, the ancient triumphal ideas were revived. No one has done more for their popularization among the learned than Petrarch (1304-74) with his famous *Trionfi.* In this work, which he wrote to free himself from his deep depression after the death of Laura, he plays on the similarity between her name and the laurel (laurus) of the triumphator. It consists of a sequence of triumphs in which the victor of each part becomes the victim of the one who follows him. Thus, Love has to bow to Chastity, who is overcome by Death; Death is vanquished by Fame, who in turn is annihilated by Time, until finally Eternity remains. The influence of Petrarch's *Trionfi* on the arts was enormous. The work was used as a literary source for many Italian paintings, and also innumerable new triumphs were invented, historical as well as allegorical.

We are interested here merely in the Triumph of Death. Apart from being the occasional subject matter in renaissance painting, it also served as a theme for actual processions. Such a pageant took place in Florence in 1511 at a time when the people had regained their native gaiety after the severe rule of Savonarola and were still unaware of the gathering storm clouds of religious and political dissensions. Its author was Piero di Cosimo.

Vasari tells us in the *Lives of the Painters* (ed. J. Foster, London 1851, vol. 2, p. 416 seq.)

that Piero, who in his youth was often called upon to assist in the arranging of the Carnival procession, was again invited to do so in his later years.

"This show was not of a pleasing or attractive character, but, on the contrary, was altogether strange, terrible, and unexpected: it gave no small pleasure to the people nevertheless, for as in their food they sometimes prefer the sharp and bitter savours, so in their pastimes are they attracted by things horrible; and these, provided they be presented to us with art and judgment, do indeed most wonderfully delight the human heart, a truth which is made apparent from the pleasure with which we listen to the recitation of tragedy. The spectacle here alluded to was the Triumph of Death; the car was prepared in the Hall of the Pope by Piero himself, and with so much secrecy, that no breath or suspicion of his purpose got abroad, and the completed work was made known and given to view at one and the same moment. The triumphal Car was covered with black cloth, and was of vast size, it had skeletons and white crosses painted upon its surface, and was drawn by buffaloes, all of which were totally black: within the Car stood the colossal figure of Death, bearing the scythe in his hand, while around him were covered tombs, which opened at all the places where the procession halted, while those who formed it chanted lugubrious songs, when certain figures stole forth, clothed in black cloth, on these vestments the bones of a skeleton were depicted in white; the arms, breast, ribs, and legs, namely, all which gleamed horribly forth on the black beneath. At a certain distance appeared figures bearing torches, and wearing masks, presenting the face of a death's head, both before and behind; these heads of death, as well as the skeleton neck beneath them, also exhibited to view, were not only painted with the utmost fidelity to nature, but had besides a frightful expression which was horrible to behold. At the sound of a wailing summons, sent forth with a hollow moan from trumpets of muffled yet inexorable tones, the figures of the dead raised themselves half out of their tombs, and seating their skeleton forms thereon, they sang the following words, now so much extolled and admired, to music of the most plaintive and melancholy character: Dolor, pianto, e penetenzia, etc."

Mental sufferance, tears and penitence are, as it were, the Leitmotif of the New Mexican rites at Easter time. Our death cart and Piero's lugubrious procession evidently belong to the same general tradition, though we are not yet able to trace its course completely. The influence which Petrarch's *Trionfi* exerted upon the Spanish authors since the 15th c. was deep and enduring. For all its classical attire, the poem's melancholy outlook upon the vanity of earthly things is truly medieval, and it was this spirit above all which appealed to the Spaniards. Many new triumphs, in literature as well as in pageantry, were patterned after the great Italian model. Finally, in the 16th c., the *Trionfi* served as a motif for a play. It is contained in the most important monument of the Spanish religious drama, a codex of 96 pieces which were written between 1550 and 1575. Its title reads: *Aucto de los Trionofos de Petrarca (a lo divino)*. In this play the triumphant Death appears on the stage riding in a cart which is drawn by Abraham, Absalom, Alexander, and Hercules. Significantly enough, the lines which Death has to speak, recall strongly the medieval Dance Macabre, which in Spain still enjoyed a wide popularity during the 16th c. How the Triumph of Death became detached from the rest of the *Trionfi*, and through what stages it passed until it became, in a greatly simplified form, part of the New Mexican Easter ritual, we are unable to say. All of the extant Spanish plays and poems of the 16th c. which deal with Death are based on the idea of the dance, and consequently do not concern us here. However, it is interesting to note that at least one of these pieces, Diego Sánchez's *Farsa de la Muerte*, was written to be performed at Easter (ca. 1536).

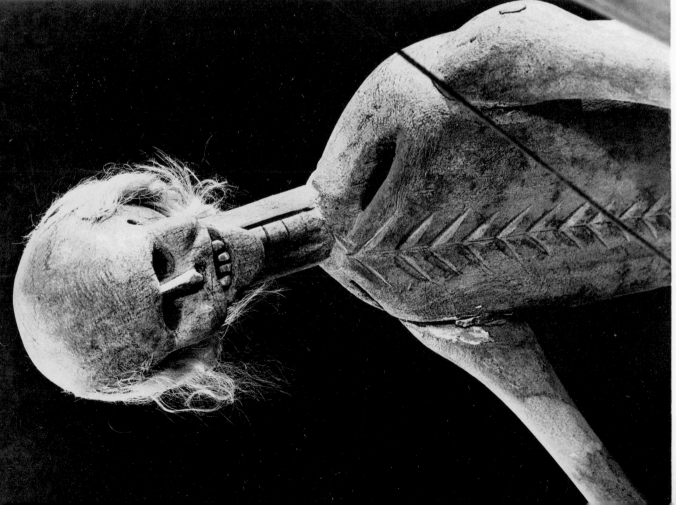

Many of these short religious plays were never meant to be printed. What has been preserved of this literature is only a fraction of the original production. The fact that there is no death play among them which uses the triumph as a motif, does not exclude the possibility of its existence. The Spaniards brought the custom of combining church celebrations with theatrical performances to the New World. We have shown how closely these two elements are interwoven in the Easter rites of New Mexico (cf. p. 38 and pl. 26). Since the ritual of the Penitente Brotherhood has its origin in that of the Third Order of St. Francis, we may assume that the idea of the New Mexican death cart was derived from the same source.

The theological and artistic development of the Death motif in the New World, outside New Mexico, is still a largely undisclosed chapter. Some light, however, is shed on the problem by a wooden figure of Death which Baltasar Gavilán, the outstanding Peruvian sculptor of the 18th c., made for the Holy Week procession of the monks of San Agustín (cf. M. Solá, *Historia del Arte hispano-americano,* 1935, fig. 110 and p. 228-29). This work, which is conceived in the spirit of the Dance of Death, shows a standing withered corpse shooting an arrow. An interesting anecdote, recalling a legend told about the New Mexican Death cart (cf. p. 40) is connected with the statue. It is reported that when, one night, the artist entered the room in which he kept his work, he was so struck by its sight that he suddenly fell dead.

A word must be said about the bow and arrow of our death figure. The vast majority of the European representations of Death shows him with a scythe, the ancient attribute of Chronos, while bow and arrow are exceedingly rare (cf. the few examples mentioned by F. Whyte, p. 134, and by J. B. Knipping, p. 107 seq.). The weapon does, however, occur rather frequently in Spanish dramatic literature (cf. D. Sánchez, *Farsa de la Muerte,* 1536; P. de Acevedo, *Comedia Caropus,* 1565 [Whyte, p. 134]; S. de Horozco, *Coloquio de la Muerte* [Whyte, p. 91]). This fact helps, therefore, to support our assumption that the death cart originated in the theater. Besides, bow and arrow fitted well into the New Mexican scene, where the Indian archer constituted a threat for anybody's life.

Our death cart comes from the village of Córdova, New Mexico. According to an oral report, it was made by the grandfather of José Lopez (cf. pl. 45). Since Lopez died in 1938, approximately sixty years of age, the cart was probably made around the middle of the 19th c. Lopez and his father were carpenters by trade. It seems likely that the grandfather followed the same calling, for the cart shows an exceptionally high degree of craftsmanship. Only wooden pegs and thongs of hide have been used for the joining of the pieces. The figure, on the other hand, is more characteristic of a highly talented autodidact than of a trained santero. The wood is thinly coated with gesso and painted with light brown. No attempt has been made to render the skeleton anatomically correct; yet no realism could have achieved a more terrifying effect. The disproportion between head and limbs is appalling. Peppino Mangravite has called the extremities spiderlike; they certainly have the appearance of a repulsive insect. While other Death figures aim with their arrows straight ahead, that is to say at the man who pulls the cart, this one threatens the spectators who watch the procession along the roadside. As a result of this arrangement, body and arms create a multiplicity of axes which in turn emphasizes the incongruity of the proportions. The head is so frightening because its tiny size is outside normal experience, and thus the fear cannot easily be rationalized. Unkempt gray hair flutters around the bald head. The thin braid which hangs down the neck only stresses the untidy appearance. The grinning mouth, the empty eyes, and half decayed nose give the features an indescribable expression of sly cruelty. This Death is truly inhuman.

[*Height of figure: 36"; total height: 51"*]

Among the New Mexican santos there are a great number of figures representing the Christ child, either with the globe in His hand, or in an attitude of benediction. His body is nude except for small trunks. These figures are called by the local people Niño Perdido or Niño de Prague. We are unable to give an exact explanation of this name. It is, however, possible to describe the trend of ideas which has resulted in these images.

The origin of the cult of the Christ child is connected with the Franciscan movement. St. Francis' Christmas celebration in the church of Greccio, where he reenacted the scene of the nativity, is well known. The Child appeared to other saints of the order, St. Clare and St. Anthony. It is not surprising, therefore, that this veneration should have become part of the Franciscan tradition.

The early 16th c. brought a new development. Detached from any narrative context the figure of the Christ child was used by wood engravers and painters on greetings cards as a symbol of the New Year. This started a trend which was to become very important in the following century.

The revelations of the great Spanish mystics to whom the Child represented a sweet mystery of innocence, gave new impetus to the cult. Under the influence of their writings, Cardinal Bérulle, undertook to renew and transform it in the beginning of the 17th c. He was soon followed by a Carmelite nun, Marguerite du Saint Sacrement, who saw the Child in a vision (1636). As a result, her native town of Beaune became a center of the new veneration. Something similar occurred in Provence, where the Christ child appeared to Jeanne Perraud, carrying the instruments of the Passion. We shall discuss in our description of pl. 60 this particular aspect of the cult in which the childhood and death of Christ are mystically linked together.

Nowhere did the veneration for the Christ child find a more fertile soil than in 17th c. France, where, as Mario Praz has pointed out, it was particularly well suited to a society which was accustomed to envisage love under the guise of the Alexandrian Eros. A revived Greek philosophic tradition thus became imbued with the Christian spirit; the Eros child was transformed into Divine Love or the Human Soul. French emblematic literature is full of scenes in which in endless variation the Christ child performs allegorical acts with these two Christianized playmates.

Religious allegorical literature of this kind spread from France to other European countries. If, therefore, our New Mexican Niños merely seem to lack wings in order to become little spiritualized love gods, it is due to this influential trend in 17th century thought.

The figure reproduced here is closely related to that on pl. 54, which apparently served as a model. The balance of the figure is somewhat uneven and the head seems to be too small in relation to the body. Yet the features are sensitive and of great charm. Hair and eyes are black. The ball shaped object which the child holds in his hand has the same design as the ornamental flowers of the board which serves the figure as a base. This ball is evidently derived from the globe, symbol of the ruler. Likewise of symbolic meaning are the wounds which the child bears on his feet.   [*Height:* 19¾"]

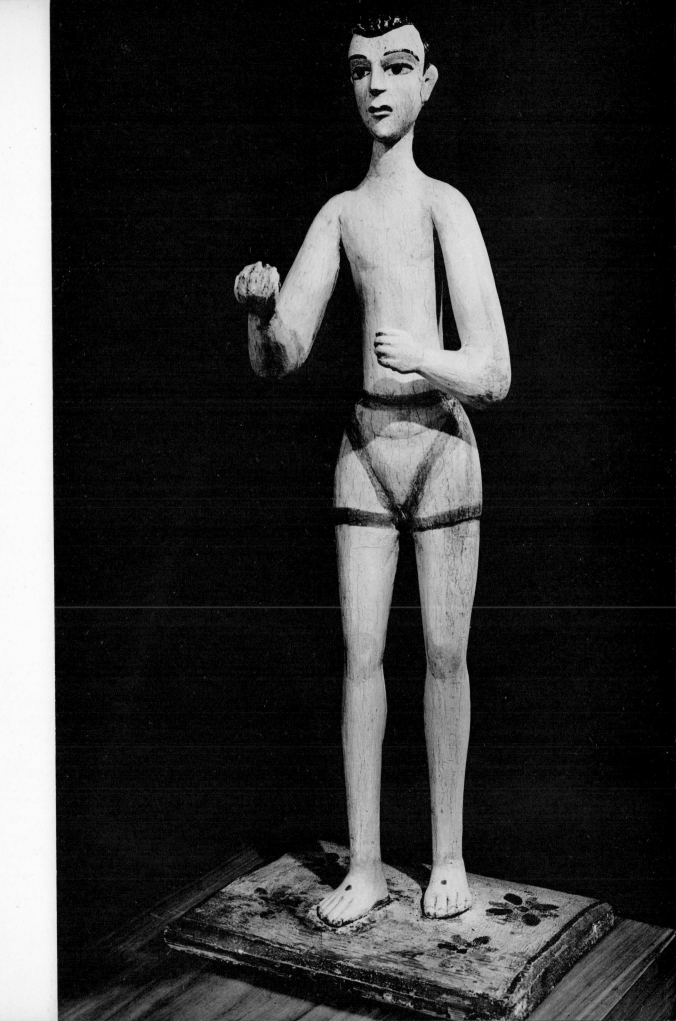

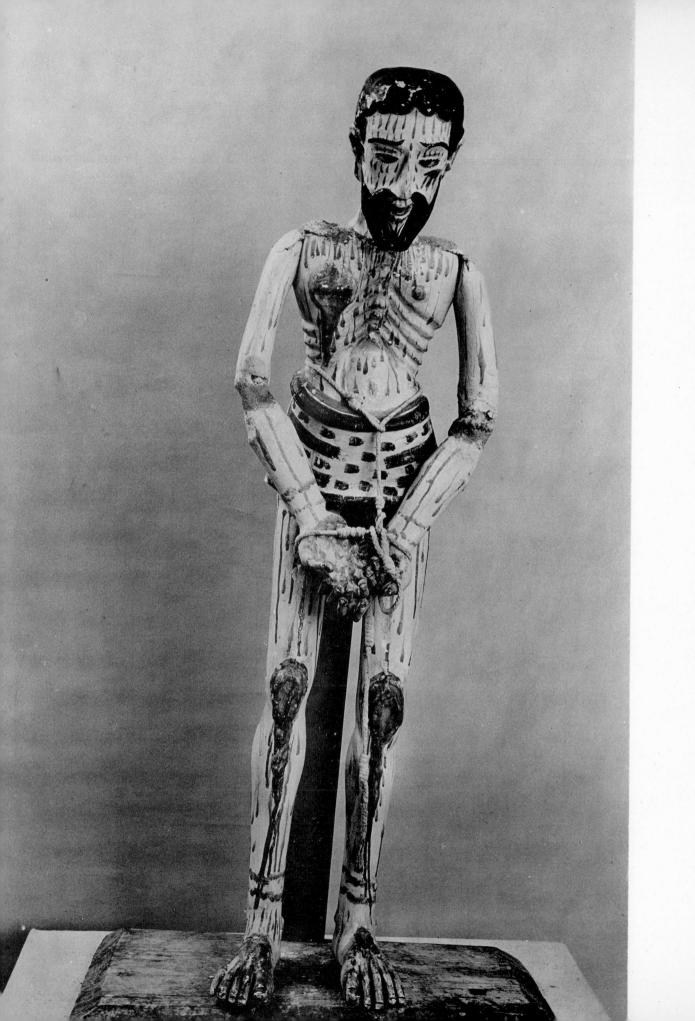

No image expresses more perfectly the sentiments of the Penitente Brothers during their severe rites than does the Man of Sorrows. Christ, who has passed through the horrors of the Passion, appears before mankind bearing the mark of His torture and the signs of indescribable anguish. He exhorts the Brothers to atone for their sins, while there is yet time. Thus the figure embodies the very idea of their religious performance, the aim of which is the imitation of Christ by means of self-inflicted pain, however great the difference may be between their own torture and the supreme sacrifice of the Saviour, and however dissimilar the motive.

The Man of Sorrows is a devotional image fashioned to create a specific mood; it does not portray any particular moment in the terrestrial existence of Christ. There are, however, scenes in His life which bear certain resemblance to this image: the Ecce Homo, that is, the derided Christ, and the Christ at the Column of Flagellation. The pictorial types of both scenes have often merged with that of the Man of Sorrows. This explains the presence of the cord around the waist of this figure and the tied hands, which do not bear the marks of the nails, in spite of the wounds in the side and on the feet.

Even the Penitente Brothers' own experiences are reflected in this Man of Sorrows. His shoulders and back are covered with wounds, that is to say, those parts of the body where the historical Christ was least hurt, but where the Penitentes concentrate their self-punishment by lashing themselves and dragging heavy crosses (cf. Lummis, *The Land of Poco Tiempo;* illus. after p. 88).

The back of the figure is remarkable for another reason. Below the left shoulder blade there is a deep oval shaped wound. Inside one can see the ribs (made of pieces of quill) and behind them the suspended heart of Christ which "palpitates" when the figure is moved. Two trends of ideas seem to have brought about this extraordinary piece of realism: the *mementi mori* of the baroque tomb statuary which indulged in the representation of half decomposed bodies, mumified corpses and skeletons, and secondly the Cult of the Sacred Heart of Christ, symbol of His divine love which, although of medieval origin, has become all important since the second half of the 17th century. We cannot refer to any comparable European work. Yet, that the Heart of Jesus cult was practised in New Mexico is proven by a number of retablos showing the Sagrado Corazón. The figure is more than half life-size. The carnation is pinkish white with some yellow spots. Bright red is used for the blood. The white loin cloth has a blue pattern and is carved of the same wood as the trunk, a customary procedure on large figures. The eyes are covered with mica plates. The pupils of the eyes are turned toward the inner angle, a very well observed detail, creating the inward and at the same time, watchful expression, of this altogether remarkable figure.

Another work by the same artist is the Ecce Homo on pl. 37.   [*Height:* 48"]

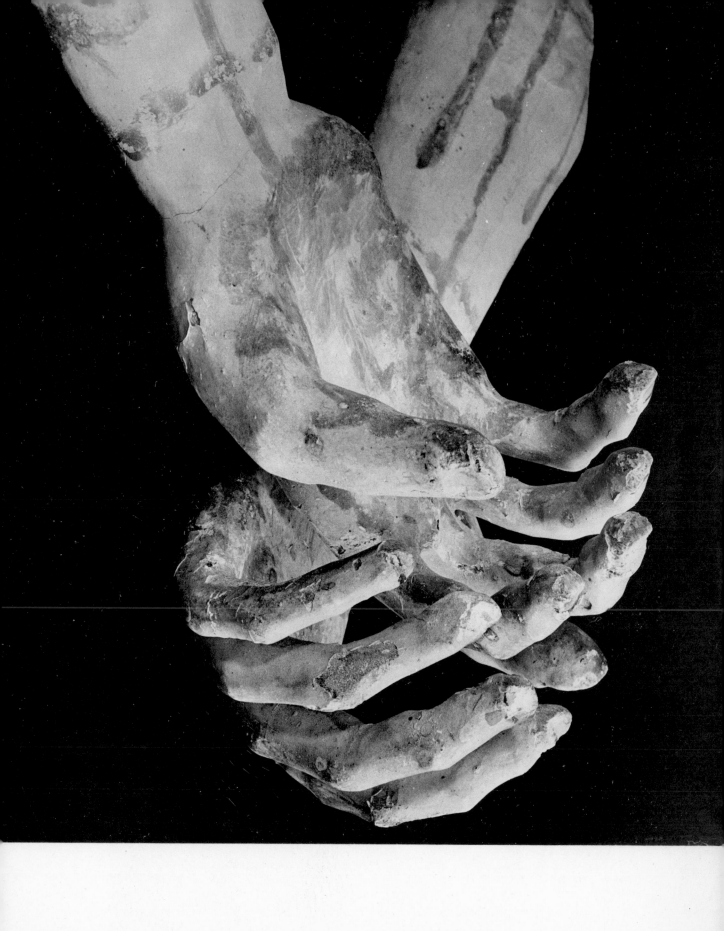

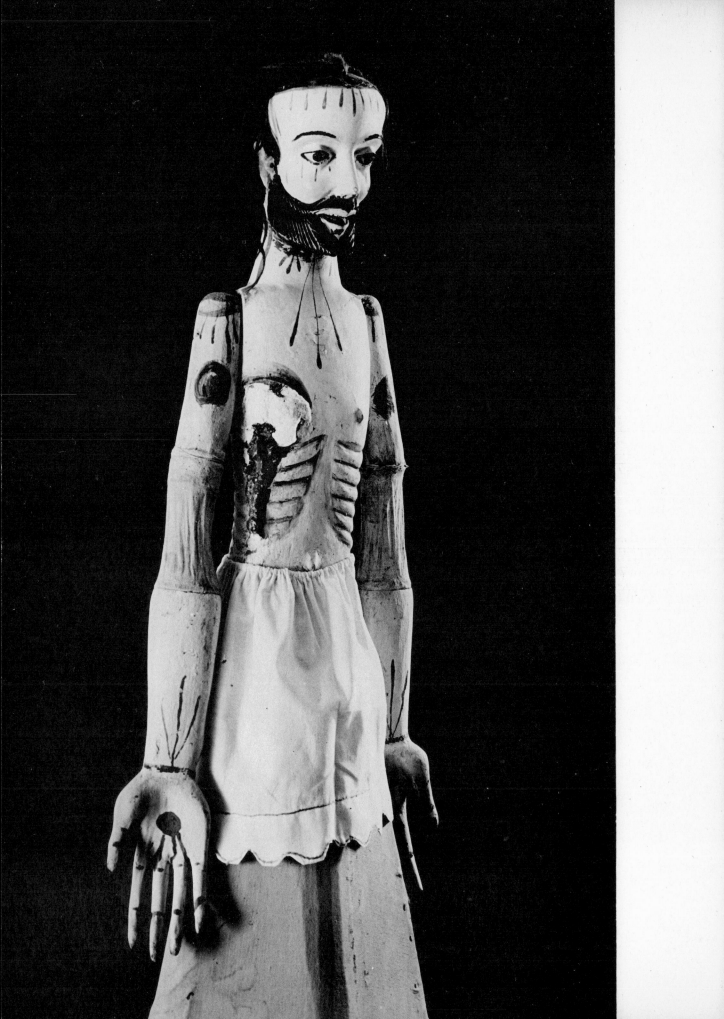

This figure of a Man of Sorrows is sculptured only in its upper half. From the hips downwards it consists of a wooden frame covered with painted blue cloth. A short apron hides the place where the frame joins the body. The joints at the elbows are made of muslin, a customary procedure for larger figures. This device is a simplified version of the flexible joints which the Spanish baroque sculptors gave the statues of this kind. (Cf. the Cross-Bearing Christ [Jesús del Gran Poder] by Montañes, 1619-1622; Sevilla, San Lorenzo. Reprod. in A. L. Mayer, Spanische Barockplastik, fig. 74 b.)

The wounds are strongly marked. Besides the usual ones on the hands and on the side, there are two more on the upper arms, possibly in order to bring their number up to the canonical five. Even the back is covered with blood. Here we can notice the reflex of actual experience; for the back is the part of the body where the Brothers of Light lash themselves in their penitential rites. The Taylor Museum possesses a photograph of such a religious performance, in which the backs of the participants are one dark area of self-inflicted wounds.

The expressiveness of the head is quite remarkable. The half-open mouth with its realistic details of teeth and tongue seems to address the worshipper under the strain of agony. We can notice similar features on the San José (pls. 18 and 19). Great care is taken in the rendering of the eyes. Their lids form a deep angle on either side of the eyeballs; the face is surmounted by a wide, bulging forehead, reminiscent of the Man of Sorrows on pl. 52. Real hair, fixed to the skull, matches the reddish-brown stylized beard. Realistic and abstract tendencies meet in this figure without harmony.   [*Height:* 45½″]

The artist of the Man of Sorrows on plate 34 also made this figure of the suffering Christ. The absence of the five wounds of the Crucifixion indicate that he wanted to show Christ in His earthly life; the figure, if dressed, represents the Ecce Homo, the derided Saviour; if undressed, Christ of the Flagellation. The ambivalence of meaning is typical of these large figures of Christ whose purpose is to reenact stages of the Passion. Just as an actor changes the character of his role with the aid of a new costume, so can these bultos take on a new significance merely by a change of their accessories. Sculpture and theater arts have merged here; in fact, there are figures which have become real puppets (cf. pls. 26 and 27).

In contrast to the Man of Sorrows, whose chest has fallen helplessly over His trunk, this figure of Christ is more erect. The head is upright. Long, unkempt curls of natural hair fall over His shoulders on both sides. In His wide open eyes there is the expression of utter bewilderment. The lips are apart, as if in speech; one can see teeth and tongue between them. The cheeks are emaciated. The play of light emphasizes their irregular planes. There is no place on which the gaze of the spectator can rest; it wanders around until it reaches the horizontal plane of the oval shaped eyes of Christ. Yet, while their form is restful, they are psychologically the very center of grave disturbances. There are few New Mexican works in which unity of form and expression are so fully realized as in this one.   [*Height: head 9″; total 58½″*]

It is often difficult to give correct names to images of the Virgin in New Mexico. Types which have a distinct meaning have sometimes been merged, as in this case. Moreover, the figure has lost its attributes which may have formerly provided a clue. The crescent painted on the skirt of the Virgin, belongs to the Immaculata, who is always represented in the attitude of prayer. On the other hand, the outstretched arm of our figure, which may have originally held a purse, is a gesture typical of the Carmel Madonna. The present state of the figure does not allow us to make any final decision.

A remarkable feature of this figure is its painting. The pale blue skirt is divided into three tiers, each of which has the same large design in red, black, dark blue, and yellow. The basic form of the pattern with centerpiece and curved side branches, is repeated in a general way by the lower part of the vest, by the shoulder and arms, and by nose and eyes. The raised brows give the face the expression of inquisitive frankness which is further stressed by the protruding upper lip and the curiously bulging chin. The facial characteristics which appropriately reappear on the Child, are typical of this craftsman (cf. pls. 48 and 54).

A pattern based on the same principle can be seen on several figures of the Virgin in Córdova, New Mexico (N. S. de Atocha; N. S. del Carmen; N. S. de la Soledad).

[Height: 24″]

In the 15th and 16th centuries the artists frequently represented the Virgin and the Child, accompanied by Elizabeth and the young John the Baptist, and sometimes St. Joseph. In the Italian High Renaissance it was one of the favorite subjects, and Raphael's timeless idyls and their many derivatives have never ceased to arouse admiration and to stimulate pious devotion.

The happy union of the two saintly families was not based on the Scriptures, but was rather the result of Franciscan meditation. It is not surprising that with the reawakened conscience in dogmatic matters which the Counter Reformation brought about, the subject became more rare. Instead, a new type was developed: the Holy Family, consisting only of the Virgin, the Child, and St. Joseph. Some artists continued to fit the group into a narrative context—e.g., Return from Egypt, or Return from the Temple—while others, like Murillo, developed it into a purely devotional image. Mary, Jesus and Joseph, the Holy Triad, is, as St. Francis of Sales called it, a Trinity on earth, counterpart of the celestial one.

The group shows unmistakably the characteristics of the santero of the "flat figures." We have previously enumerated the features peculiar to this craftsman: the flat, unmodeled bodies, the strongly conventionalized faces, and the two-colored garments which outline the front views. In this instance the front parts of the main garment of all three figures are red; the back of St. Joseph is green, that of the Virgin slate blue with yellow edges.

[*Height:* 18¾"; 8½"; 15½"]

St. Christopher, the giant, who carried the Christ child across a stream and almost collapsed under the weight of Him who created the world, rarely occurs in New Mexico. In fact, this figure is the only sculptured image of St. Christopher which has come to our knowledge thus far.

As a sign of the great physical strength of the saint, the craftsman has given him hands and feet of enormous size. He wears short green trousers with narrow parallel folds. The upper part of the body is rendered in a simplified manner which reminds one of the technique of the "flat figures." His features, on the other hand, are lively. The slightly open mouth and the squinting eyes give the giant the expression of goodhumored awkwardness.

St. Christopher, who is one of the Fourteen Holy Helpers, sees to it that those who believe in him do not die unprepared. He is, especially, the patron of travellers.   [*Height:* 24½″]

Throughout the Middle Ages the road to Compostela, where according to the legend, St. James the Greater was buried, was probably the most travelled one in all Europe. Thousands crossed the Pyrenees to his famous shrine in northwestern Spain. In fact, the Santiago pilgrim was such a well known figure in Europe, that the saint himself adopted the appearance of his venerators. On innumerable statues and paintings he wears the pilgrim's cloak, the wide hat with the shell on it, and the pilgrim's badge from the shores of Galicia.

For Spain, St. James is a national hero. In the battle of Clavijo (834), Don Ramiro had recognized him on a white horse, as he was charging against the Moors. It was due to his miraculous intervention that the battle was won.

Spanish art created the image of Santiago on horseback at an early age; he is so represented over one of the portals of his cathedral, in the 12th century. While the type is rarely found outside the country, and only at a much later date, in Spain it always remained a very popular image. The Militant Church, above all, saw in it a glorious symbol in her fight against infidels and heretics. Through the Conquest it entered the New World and eventually came to New Mexico. It was apparently the only aspect under which the saint became known in New Mexico, for while St. James the pilgrim would have meant little to the people there, Santiago Matamoro, the killer of the Moors, was a powerful protector in their own struggle on the frontier.

Our little sculpture is arresting in spite of its small size. This is the result no less of its shortcomings than of its merits. The craftsman wished to make a santo; the artistic problem of horse and rider which would have fascinated a European sculptor, was of no concern to him. On the contrary, the horse, though part of the story, is no more important than an attribute. It does not matter, therefore, whether the horse is undersized or bow legged, nor whether the head is tiny (a common feature in primitive art), so long as the saintly hero is rendered in such a manner as to attract the worshipper's whole attention. There is wisdom in this argument. The very humbleness of the animal serves to accentuate the triumphant pride of the rider, a valiant knight, Santiago and Don Quixote in one.

The fragile bulto has repeatedly been broken and repaired. One can notice the hands of several santeros, each of whom has contributed his share. As the figure appears today, it is rather the work of a group of craftsmen than that of an individual. This observation can be made also with regard to other santos.   [*Height:* 12½"]

Although derived from the same prototype as the figures of San José reproduced on pls. 17 and 18, this work presents a very different interpretation of the subject. The extreme elongation of the body in conjunction with the system of narrow, parallel folds is a means of increasing the impression of the extraordinary spiritual powers of the saint. The scarf, vestige of the prototype, has shrunk to a thin cloth which enlivens the surface of the figure without destroying its contours or interfering with the rising forces of the lines. A tendency toward abstraction prevails also in the rendering of the head. No contact between figure and onlooker is attempted, but the deep blue eyes of the saint are filled with the glow of an invisible world.

One would, of course, expect a similarly hieratic interpretation of the Christ child, yet there we face an element of surprise. Though the Child gives the sign of blessing, it pays no attention to the worshipper, but seeks tenderly to shelter against the breast of a foster father whose mind is far above the low region of mild, human emotions.

The reasons for such contradictions can be easily explained. The prototype, which was presumably thoroughly human and realistic, has been transformed into an image of transcendental character as far as the saint is concerned, while in the same process the Child remained more or less untouched. The resulting incongruities, however, only add to the fascination of this work.

The figure is heavily covered with house paint. The original color scheme may well have been different.   [*Height: 38½"*]

Plate Forty-three   NUESTRA SEÑORA DEL REFUGIO
DE PECADORES

Nuestra Señora del Refugio is a painting of Italian origin of which there are several copies in Mexico, the most celebrated one being the image in the church of the Colegio Apostólico de Guadalupe in Zacatecas. It shows the crowned Virgin in half-figure over a cloud or the crescent of the moon, holding the Child on her arm. The image became quite popular in New Mexico, for there are several retablos still in existence which have been copied from prints.

To translate a painted copy of this kind into sculptural terms was a task far beyond the abilities of the carver of this bulto. He gave the truncated image legs of the most rudimentary form, and seated it on a throne of fantastic shape. It consists of a high center part with extensions on either side. These are decorated with double volutes.

The bulto, which is painted in red, yellow, and blue, is one of the rare figures bearing a date; it was made in the year 1820.   [*Height:* 21″; *figure with throne* 16½″]

This charming figure of a little boy seems far removed from the usual conception of a powerful archangel who fights the devil. Indeed, the delicate child with bare knees and short garment has a closer resemblance to San Rafael, who in New Mexican art often adopts the features of the young Tobias (cf. pl. 21). Yet in spite of these apparent incongruities and although attributes are missing, the faded painting on the pedestal provides us with a clue for the identification. There one can recognize two heads, one of which is turned upside down. These are the fallen angels on their way to Hell. A very similar figure in the Cathedral Museum of Santa Fe confirms this interpretation. On the pedestal of this statue there are two carved heads in the same position as on our piece. The similarity goes even farther. The gestures, especially the rendering of the hands, are identical. Over an armour which covers breast and trunk, the Cathedral figure is wearing a skirt of fanciful cut which is lifted by the wind. This garment is an awkward copy of a prototype from which the pleated skirt on our figure is also derived. In Santa Fe one of the attributes, the sword, is still preserved; the second, however, the scales, which St. Michael was holding in his left hand, has disappeared. Our figure has completely lost the baroque character which the other one has kept to some degree. In its place, it has gained the stylistic purity and the directness of true folk art.

The expression, as well as the form of the face, are quite similar to those of the Virgin on pl. 12. It is not unlikely that both figures were made by the same man.

The legend of St. Michael has been discussed on pl. 28.

[*Height of figure: 27½″; total height: 34½″*]

This group of St. Michael fighting the Devil is the most recent work illustrated in this volume, and is the only figure to be signed with the name of its author, José Dolores Lopez of Córdova, New Mexico.

Like his father and his grandfather, who presumably made the Death Cart (pls. 30 to 32), Lopez was a carpenter by trade. He was much respected in his community and ranked high in the Penitente Order. He died in 1938, approximately sixty years of age, as the result of an automobile accident, and was buried in the yard of the old Mission at Córdova, an honor granted to few. His grave is marked by a cross which he had made himself and had kept for years in his house.

Lopez mastered his craft with great skill. He made highly ornamented chests, beds, tables and decorative screen door frames. During the long winter months he used to carve small animals, such as birds and squirrels, a work in which the whole family participated. The uncomplicated animal forms which he chose gave him an opportunity to apply the rich ornamentation of which he was a master.

In his most ambitious work, San Miguel, Lopez indulges to the full in the technical aspects of his craft. Failure to paint the bulto reveals weaknesses that may be true of many of the santos, had they likewise been left in the native wood. There can be little doubt that this figure of the great archangel fails in its expression of popular devotion to the saint. The statue becomes a purposeful endeavour of one man unable to transmit the essentials of true folk art.

[Height of San Miguel: 44″; *length of Devil:* 35″]

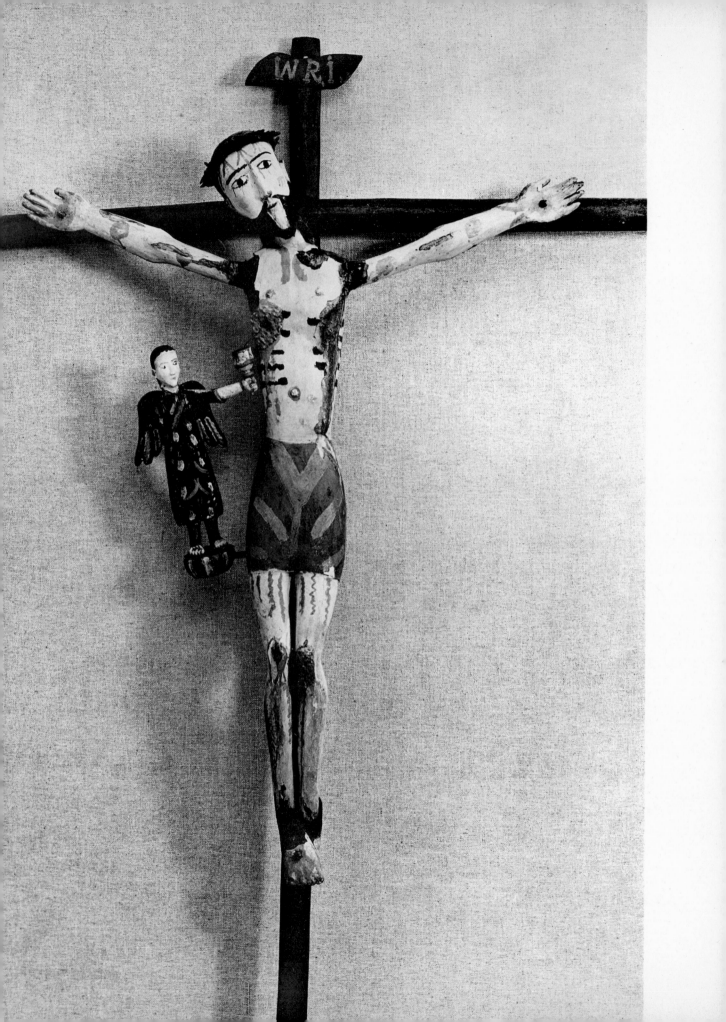

Beside the dignified, quiet crucifix on pls. 50 and 51, and the realistic expression of that on pl. 23, this crucifix appears extremely awkward. It is a perfect specimen of a crude and sincere folk art. The forms of the body are strongly conventionalized. More complicated details, such as toes, are merely outlined. Painting had to complete what the sculptor was unable to represent. Unfortunately, the last restorer to lay hands on the bulto chose rather unpleasing colors. He used a strong pink for the flesh tints of the body, a brilliant red for the blood marks, blue for the loin cloth and for the ribs. While this new paint cover has considerably changed the appearance of the work, the head at least has remained more or less untouched, and thus gives us an idea of what was originally intended.

The pear-shaped head is treated in the same flat manner which has been used for the body. The painting is reminiscent of peasant dolls; a pinkish white is used for the carnation, red for the spots on the cheeks, black for the eyes and the pointed beard.

Just as in a fairy tale the fantastic and the real are interwoven inseparably, so in folk art are abstract and realistic elements. Therefore, the disarming simplicity of the work does not exclude the use of an iconographic device of pronounced realism. The deep wound in the side of Christ is filled with a wick which presumably at Eastertide was soaked with a red liquid. A wire led the drops into a cup which the little angel is holding. This feature is not at all rare in New Mexico; the crucifix on pl. 23, for example, is treated in exactly the same manner. Moreover, the Taylor Museum possesses cup-bearing angels which undoubtedly had this function on some crucifix. We shall discuss the religious meaning of this motif on pl. 64.   [*Height of Christ:* 36″; *height of angel:* 10½″]

This santo was done in a technique which was used sometimes for larger figures. The pattern of the stiff ceremonial skirt has been painted on cloth which had been previously dipped in gesso, and stretched over a wooden frame. The arms are flexible in the joints. The mica eyes, the red tints on the cheeks and the fat chin, and especially the half-open mouth give the face a very lively expression. These features have been noted already on the Mater Dolorosa (pl. 4), which almost certainly was made by the same man.

The identification of this santo is based on the painted rosary which she wears around her neck. The rosary was one of the most important spiritual weapons of the Counter Reformation in fighting the heretics. Even though the Dominican Order has always cherished the belief that the virtues of the rosary were revealed to its great founder, historical evidence proves that the cult in its present form was instituted and zealously propagated in the second half of the 15th c. by the Dominican preacher Alanus van der Clip (de la Roche). The rosary had its greatest triumph when Pope Pius V attributed to the intervention of Our Lady of the Rosary the naval victory of Lepanto (1571), which rescued Europe from the Turks. The day on which the battle was fought has been celebrated by the Church ever since as the feast of Our Lady of the Rosary. Powerful in the fight against the infidel, the rosary is also "a chain which links Heaven and earth," as Saint Teresa called it; it is a means of salvation for the souls of the living and of the deceased alike.   [*Height:* 38"]

A comparison of this bulto with the figure of Our Lady on pl. 38 reveals that both are unquestionably by the same hand. The features of the face, its bulging chin and jowl, the
puckered lips, and the little bumps on the ridge of the nose, are remarkably alike. Both wear
the same short red jacket over a slate blue undergarment. The gestures are also identical.

There are a few minor differences. The moon is sculptured, while it was merely painted on
the other figure. The Virgin wears a crown. The Child, whose gestures are more lively, is
here shown in the nude except for red trunks.

Another work of the same santero is the Niño on pl. 54.   [*Height including crown:* 45″]

The pictorial rendering of the Holy Trinity has presented great problems to the Christian artists. The idea of a threefold Deity is essentially spiritual and seems to defy translation into visual forms.

Among the various types which were created in the course of time, the one most generally adopted depicts God the Father and God the Son in the shape of human beings, while the Holy Spirit is represented under the symbol of the dove.

For centuries this type competed with another concept which had originated in Byzantium. It took as its basis a passage from the first chapter of Genesis, where God on the sixth day of the Creation announces His resolution with the words: "Let us make man in our image, after our likeness." (Genesis 1:26.) The sudden change of speech from the singular, hitherto used, to the plural, startled the theologians who interpreted the passage as meaning that the creation was the work of the Holy Trinity, not of the Father alone. If, however, man was created after the likeness of the Trinity, it was logical to conclude that the threefold Deity bore the features of man. Therefore, one represented the Trinity under the image of three men with identical features. This Byzantine type was brought to Western Europe during the Middle Ages and continued to flourish there well into the 18th century, when Pope Benedict XIV forbade these images in the Constitution of 1745. While this papal decree was obeyed in Europe—a famous altar piece in Baden near Vienna was sold for this reason—it apparently never reached New Mexico. There this heretical type was used along with the officially approved version.

The iconography of the retablo offers another peculiar feature: the bodies of the three holy persons are shown grown together. With this device which originated in the 13th century, the artists meant to express the idea that the Holy Trinity is threefold and one at the same time. The chain which links the three persons together serves the same purpose. This motif occurs already in a Flemish manuscript from circa 1415, as Dr. Erwin Panofsky has kindly pointed out to us. (Cf. Leroquais, *Un Livre d'Heures de Jean sans Peur,* 1939, pl. XIV.)

[*Height:* 10″]

The spirit of peace emanates from this crucifix. The lean body of Christ is not contorted under the stress of pain, but stretches limply upon the cross. There is no struggle between the stiff forms of the wood and the pliant forms of the body. The head is leaning forward rather than falling over the breast. Eyes and mouth are half open. There is sadness in the face, not the reflex of physical torture, as generally depicted.

The figures of the Virgin and of St. John are both shown frontally and with identical gestures. Their size is dwarflike if compared to that of Christ. They pray piously at a moment when the expression of extreme horror and grief would be natural. This may seem incongruous. Yet in these figures, two originally distinct ideas may have been merged: the representation of the historical witnesses of the Crucifixion, the Virgin and St. John, and of the donors of the image who appear in the attitude of quiet prayer and, as a sign of humility, in a considerably smaller size than the holy persons. This arrangement is quite in keeping with the spirit of the whole work which stresses the symbolic meaning of the sacrifice instead of displaying its historical setting. The worshipper is asked to concentrate wholly upon the suffering Christ.

This crucifix is singularly free of the two conflicting tendencies in New Mexican art: folk art abstraction, and the inherited realism of the Spanish Baroque. Instead it seems that the prototype of our crucifix belongs to the late Gothic period of Spanish art, when the national characteristics, especially the trend toward realism, had not yet been developed. If this assumption be true, it would explain also the stylistic uniformity of the group, for a late Medieval work was closer to the New Mexican artist's own expression than the elaborate Baroque which, of necessity, had to be submitted to a process of simplification. A grayish yellow has been used for the flesh tints of the crucifix. The representation of Christ with the pallor of the grave is unique in New Mexico, though quite customary in Mexico. The loin cloth is yellow and brown, the crown is green, the dress of Mary is red upon yellow, that of St. John is red, with his coat of light yellow.

The rendering of the loin cloth occurs commonly in New Mexican art, consisting of a piece of cloth covered with gesso, and bow carved in wood in order to give it the necessary stiffness. (Cf. pl. 64.)   [*Height of Christ: 36"; Height of Virgin and St. John: 11½"*]

There is hardly a more terrifying theme in Christian art than the Man of Sorrows; the Christ after His Passion, who appears before the faithful as a living corpse. Nor is there an image which could stir up the soul and evoke the desire for penance more strongly. This is subject matter which expresses to the fullest the spirit of the Penitente Brotherhood of New Mexico. It can be assumed with certainty that this bulto was made for one of these societies.

European images of the Man of Sorrows tend predominantly towards realism, which at times take on extreme and even brutal forms. Our craftsman, on the other hand, wisely recognizing his own technical limitations, goes in the opposite direction; he stylizes. By means of abstract forms he creates a truly ghost-like apparition which expresses more convincingly the co-existence of life and death than any realistic treatment could have achieved.

From the iconographic point of view it may be surprising to see a Man of Sorrows whose body is not naked except for the loin cloth. One has to consider, however, that the New Mexicans customarily dress their santos. Therefore, they would hardly find anything unusual in this type. There is, moreover, another technical reason: the simple forms of our figure could be carved more easily.

The body of the figure and the lower and upper arm are made of solid wood. For the joints of the arms, cloth is used. The whole figure is built up with abstract forms of rhomboid shape, one of which represents the lower part of the body, followed by others for breast, shoulders, neck, chin and mouth, cheekbones and skull. The wounds on hands and feet and in the face are stylized in a similar mathematical manner. The peruke of natural hair which contrasts so strangely with the abstract style of the figure, is presumably a gift of a pious worshipper. The facial expression is particularly fascinating. We have met it elsewhere, on the San Rafael (pls. 15 and 16). There can hardly be any doubt that both were made by the same master. The strange shape of the ears on both figures represents his unmistakable signature.

[Height: 34″]

St. Isidore, the ploughman, is the patron of the farmer and the protector of the crops, a function which gives him an important place among the New Mexican saints.

His gradual rise to sainthood and general veneration is paralleled by the slow but steady process through which the peasants, lowest of the social groups of Europe, became conscious of their need and their role in society.

San Ysidro's model life was spent on a farm outside Madrid where he died in 1130. His memory was kept alive in that region and more than a hundred years later, at the time when the disciples of St. Francis and St. Dominic preached the virtues of poverty, his life story was written down (ca. 1261). Again, it took centuries before he was admitted to the hierarchy of intermediaries between God and mankind. In 1622 he was canonized together with companions of a very different character: SS. Ignatius, Francis Xavier, Teresa, and Philip Neri. And while these exponents of the Militant Church were shining brilliantly in the century of the Thirty Years' War, there grew up in Germany the cult of the true counterpart of San Ysidro, that of the humble Notburga, beloved patron of the maidservants.

The life of San Ysidro, devoted to work, charity, and prayer, is, of necessity, lacking in the dramatic highlights of those of other saints. By legend, it is said of him that angels did the work for him while he was praying. It is in this aspect that he is usually represented in New Mexico.

New Mexican religious art is almost completely un-narrative, and this group is no exception. Although the figures of the saint, the angel behind the plow, and the oxen, which do their work with such moving expression of pious patience, relate a story in accordance with the legend, the difference in scale tells us that angel and animals must be interpreted as attributes.

Considering the difficulties which the elaborate iconography presented, the artist has solved his task admirably. Instead of rendering a genre piece as his contemporary European colleague would have done, he created a work of dignity and religious significance.

[*Height of main figure 21½"; Height of small figures 11¾"*]

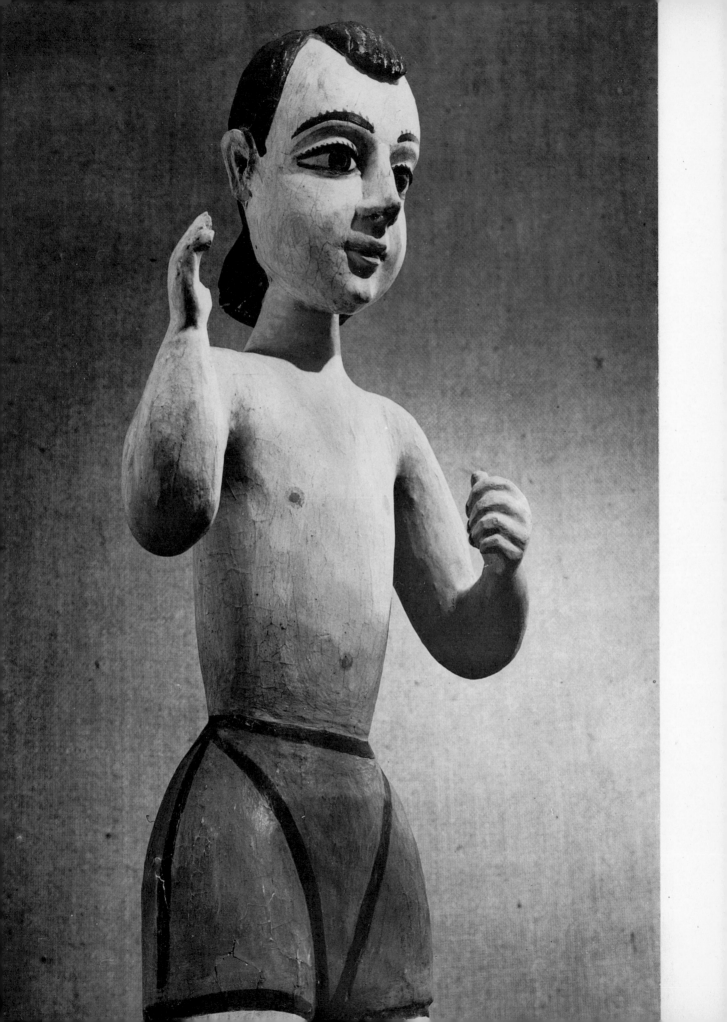

The trend of religious ideas which produced the images of the Christ child has already been discussed in connection with the Niño illustrated on pl. 33. That figure is closely related to the accompanying bulto, whose artistic qualities are considerably higher. The New Mexican santero was rarely able to form the youthful human body so convincingly. The proportions are correct. The figure stands firmly on its feet with legs apart. The sculptor has enlivened the customary frontality by giving the main axis of the figure a slight twist and allowing the direction of the feet to diverge, rather than placing them parallel to one another.

The Child gives the sign of benediction. He wears light blue trunks, with green and brown stripes. The body shows the "sunburn" tints not only on the joints of the limbs, but on feet, upper arms, chest, and back. The attribute which He formerly held in His left hand, is now lost.

The head is remarkable for its vivid expression and delicate coloring. Hair, eyebrows, and eyelashes are of the same subdued brown color which was used for the pattern on the trunks, while the blue reappears in a grayish hue in the coloring of the wide open eyes. The full cheeks and the little round chin contrast strongly with the bold nose. We have seen these characteristics on other figures. The images of Our Lady on pls. 38 and 48 are evidently by the same artist.   [*Height: 27½"*]

This picture of the seated Virgin presenting the Child in ceremonial manner in strict frontality, is a fairly exact rendering of a celebrated Spanish image of the Madonna, Nuestra Señora del Camino in Pamplona (cf. fig. 3).

Both Mother and Child are dressed in heavy cloaks which hide the body so completely that by merely looking at the picture it would be impossible to tell whether the figures are seated or standing. The peculiar headgear framing their faces is the result of a misinterpretation of the prototype. In the latter the heads are veiled with a cloth, which leaves merely a window-like opening for the face. The rims of the opening are decorated with metal work. This detail has been preserved on the retablo, while the veil has been omitted. Another instance of misinterpretation is the leaf the Virgin holds in her hands, which represents a scepter. The moon, which the retablo has in common with the original in Pamplona and which belongs iconographically to the Immaculata, was added to the Pamplona image during the Post-Renaissance period.

The flowers, the curtain, and the two angels are obviously space fillers, presumably invented by the painter or engraver who copied the sculptured image.

Among her venerated images of the Virgin, Spain possesses several which bear the name Nuestra Señora del Camino. While they vary in age and in type (the image of León, for example, is a Pietà), they are all so called because they are preserved in churches which lie on a road of foremost importance, the Camino de Santiago. (Cf. pl. 41.)

[*Measurements:* 20½" x 15⅝"]

The discoveries of the 16th century widened the world enormously. Regions that had hitherto been known to Europe merely through fantastic reports now became geographic realities. As soon as the Church had recovered from the blows of the Reformation, the modern heroic age of the missions began. The militant Jesuits were the leaders. St. Francis Xavier went to India, then proceeded to Japan, where he landed in 1549. His activities bore immense fruit; at the time of his death there were 200,000 Christians and 250 churches in the country. Indeed, the Christianization of Japan was so extensive that it caused a counter-movement to grow which was bitterly opposed to this early form of westernization. The first severe blow against the Christian was struck in 1596. It happened that a ship, one of the Manila galleons, coming from the Philippines and bound for Mexico, stranded on the Nipponese shores in July of that year. Since there were soldiers and missionaries on board, the rumor spread that an invasion had been planned in which the clergymen were acting merely as decoys for the military. Emperor Taicosama, who was ill-disposed towards the Christians, had the priests arrested and tortured, together with other religious, twenty-six in all. In February, 1597 there were taken to Nagasaki, tied to crosses and pierced with spears. One of these men who died heroically for their faith was San Felipe de Jesús, member of the Franciscan mission in the Philippines. He and his companions were the forerunners of the 52 martyrs of 1622 and of the thousands who were killed in a wholesale slaughter in 1637. In 1640 Japan was closed to foreigners for more than two centuries.

This retablo has been carried out in a very simple, yet most convincing manner. The figure was first outlined; afterwards the garment, hair, and beard were filled in in black. The two lances behind the saint and the gesture of the outstretched arms are symbolic of his martyrdom. San Felipe de Jesús has become a patron saint of his native town, Mexico City, a fact which may explain his cult in New Mexico.   [*Measurements:* 14″ x 11¾″]

As a rule the New Mexican artists represent the Holy Trinity in the shape of three identical persons (cf. pl. 49). Rarely do they choose other types. On this retablo we see the Man of Sorrows lying in the lap of God the Father, while over His head the dove of the Holy Spirit descends.

This type originated in France in the second half of the 14th century. Contemporary records refer to it as Pitié-de-Nostre-Seigneur. It gives expression to the thought that the all-loving God does not remain unmoved by the suffering of His son, but takes part in it with profound pity. Iconographically, the type is derived from the German Pietà, the Virgin holding her dead son in her lap. In these German devotional images which originated around 1300, the desire to experience mystically the Passion of Christ has found its fullest expression.

From France the Pitié-de-Nostre-Seigneur spread to the neighboring countries. Along with other medieval themes it was adopted by the baroque artists. We find it among the work of Rubens and of Ribera, to cite a Spanish example.

Our retablo is noteworthy for its color scheme. God the Father wears a red cloak over a white undergarment. The triangular space around Him is filled with bright orange which changes to red where it reaches the gray clouds. Beyond these the ground is greenish blue. The plane of the foreground is black. This arrangement by which a dark outer frame surrounds a luminous center suggests that the composition has been derived from some illusionistic baroque model; Guido Reni's Immaculata for S. Biagio in Forlì, for instance, is based on very similar principles.   [*Measurements:* 11½" x 8½"]

We have included this retablo as a specimen of a technique which combines painting and sculpture. The sculptural forms have been modeled in gesso on the wooden panel. After drying, relief and background have been painted or glazed in various colors. The most striking features of the elevated parts are the many curved planes and sharp ridges. This panel has been repainted, using commercial oil paint.

The technique of modeling in low relief appears as a minor development in New Mexican folk art. The talents of the artist were restricted by the difficulties of the medium, and relief retablos are generally lacking in the freedom of expression found in painting. While the present example is carried out entirely in relief, in other retablos of this type there is often a limited use of modeling to emphasize one particular feature of the saint, the remainder being executed in the more adaptable brush-work.

The composition has been derived from the center panel of the reredos of 1760 which formerly stood in the Castrense chapel in Santa Fe, and which is now in the church of Cristo Rey (Santa Fe). The cult of "Our Lady of Light" is connected with the Portuguese Franciscans who in 1516 founded in her honor a mission in India (diocese of St. Thomas of Mylapore, Goa). St. Francis Xavier, the great Jesuit missionary, seems to have enrolled himself and his companions in a confraternity of "Our Lady of Light" before sailing for India in 1540.

The cult gained new importance in Sicily in the early part of the 18th century. At that time political disturbances alienated many people from the Church. Eager to strengthen the Sicilians in their faith, the Jesuit Father Giovanni Antonio Genovessi sought the advice of a holy nun. It is reported that the Virgin of Light answered the prayers of this nun by appearing to her in a vision. The apparition was painted by an artist according to the description of the nun. The painting was brought to Mexico by the Jesuits who, in 1732, erected a shrine in honor of Nuestra Señora de la Luz in their church (now Cathedral) in León. The image, which is still venerated there, is the prototype of all subsequent replicas.

The cult of Our Lady of Light gained wide popularity in Mexico as is testified by numerous churches and chapels dedicated to her. A splendid sanctuary was built in Puebla in 1761. Its façade is decorated with tiled pictures, one of which represents Our Lady of Light, while another depicts San Joseph de la Luz, an image patterned after the former. (Reprod. in E. A. Cervantes, *Loza Blanca y Azulejo de Puebla*. Mexico, 1939, vol. II, p. 130-135).

The center of the retablo here reproduced is taken up by a large figure of the Virgin and Child standing on a cloud, supported by angels. Two cherubs are holding a crown over her head. With her right hand the Virgin draws a soul out of the jaws of a monster, while on her left an angel, with a gesture of adoration, offers to her and the Child a vessel filled with flaming hearts. The symmetry of the composition is quite appropriate for a devotional image.

The pictorial representation of Purgatory appeared as late as the end of the Middle Ages and only in the scene of the "Mass of St. Gregory." Under the influence of the great religious controversies, however, it became a favorite subject matter since the last decade of the 16th c. There are numerous baroque paintings which depict the liberation of souls from the flames of Purgatory. It is interesting to note that as a rule the Virgin assists her Son in this act of merciful intercession. In fact, the confident belief that the Mother of Christ will come to the aid of the sinner is so strong that some painters portray only the Virgin in this scene, either alone, or with the Child on her arm.

The image of the Virgin of Light belong to this latter iconographic type. If its occurrence is relatively uncommon in New Mexico, it is presumably because of the wide popularity of the Carmelite Madonna, an image which expresses the same belief and which is, moreover, endowed with great indulgences.   [*Measurements:* 22" x 16"]

Like a block print, this picture is conceived in a graphic manner with no indication of three dimensional space. The figure is built up by means of lines and flat color planes. Black is used for the biretta, the sleeves, the ermine tails, and the cross; red on the lining of the cloak (collar and sleeves), on the body of Christ and for the background pattern; the branch around the cross is grey, hair and eyes are brown. There is a fine, unspoiled feeling for design. The picture plane is divided into three tiers by the rudimentary horizon and the upper edges of the cloak. The only forceful diagonal is introduced by the cross, which receives its due accent in this manner. The head is framed by a halo of fine red lines, a motif which is repeated in black on the border, while the feather motif on the semicircular extension of the frame gives emphasis to the composition as a whole.

For centuries John Nepomuk was a local hero in Bohemia. As a holder of a high ecclesiastical office he defended the rights of the Church against the unjustified demands of King Wenceslaus IV, who personally subjected him to torture. In his capacity as the Queen's confessor, St. John refused to reveal the secrets of the confessional, which the king tried in vain to extract from him. The king finally caused him to be drowned in the Moldau river in 1383.

Although his memory was kept in great honor among the people, his rise to universal fame began only at a time when the Church was in need of new heroes. The Jesuits rediscovered him. One of their members, Bohuslaus Balbinus, wrote down the legend of St. John in 1670. Subsequently, he was proclaimed a martyr of the Sacrament of Penance. A powerful symbol in the fight of the Jesuits against the Hussite heretics of Bohemia, his cult spread rapidly. In 1728 he was solemnly admitted into the hierarchy of saints.

Images of St. John are very numerous, especially in the countries formerly ruled over by the Hapsburg family. Until this day, travellers who pass through Czechoslovakia, Austria, and Bavaria may notice his statues on hundreds of bridges, for the saint who has perished by drowning is by reverse analogy a powerful protector against floods.

The iconography of our retablo is simple. The saint wears the garment of a canon. Apart from the palm branch of a martyr, his attribute is significantly a crucifix, for this symbol of ascetic life reflects most perfectly the mood of an age which was torn by religious struggles.

[*Measurements of the square:* 20″ x 16½″]

The cult of the Christ child reached its climax in the 17th c. (cf. pl. 33). While originally merely the joyful sides of Christ's early childhood were stressed, later the worshipper's delight in the innocence of the infant is tempered by the request that he be mindful of His future fate. He is asked to contemplate the childhood of Christ under the aspect of His Passion.

Since the 15th c., therefore, one can often observe in works of art how the Christ child turns away from the Virgin who is holding Him, in order to look seriously at the cross staff of the little John the Baptist, or at the crown of thorns and the nails which angels present to Him. At times He is depicted carrying the implements of His Passion, at others, He has fallen asleep on a cross, or is engaged in binding a crown of thorns, well aware of the implications of His task (Murillo).

These ideas have reached New Mexico from Spain. They are expressed in the Niño on pl. 33 whose feet are marked with the nail wounds. They are also present in this retablo.

The picture is divided into two halves. Above we see the Virgin and St. Joseph on either side of the Child. All of them hold a branch with a flower in one hand. Curiously enough the painter has given two halos to the parents, a plane one, as well as one the form of which is derived from the metal nimbs applied to statues. The red, crater-shaped object on which the Child stands is a chalice, symbolic container of Christ's blood. A retablo in the collection of Mr. G. Espinosa is the means of our interpreting the scene as a Presentation of Christ in the Temple. There the Child is seated on the rim of a vessel resembling a baptismal font. He blesses with His right hand, and holds in His left a heart surmounted by a cross. (Cf. *New Mexico Magazine*. April 1935, p. 23.)

The scene underneath again shows the Virgin, but with her eyes closed as a sign of grief. On the right stands St. John the Baptist, while the center is occupied by a cross on which the shroud is hanging. The meaning of this scene is evidently a symbolic crucifixion. Such abbreviated representations of the Crucifixion occur also as separate subject matter. The Taylor Museum possesses a retablo which shows a shrouded cross of identical shape.

The supreme sacrifice of Christ, through which mankind is freed from the bondage of sin, is an act of Redemption. So is the Presentation in the Temple. As Dr. Erwin Panofsky has kindly pointed out to us, there are two ritual acts combined in the Biblical report of the Presentation (Luke II, 22-24): the sacrifice of pigeons by the mother for purification (Leviticus XII), and the redemption of the first-born boy by the father. According to the Mosaic law the first-born boy belongs to God and therefore has to be redeemed thirty days after his birth by offering five shekels in money, or its equivalent in valuables. If we are correct in our interpretation, the Presentation would typologically prefigure the Crucifixion. That the Presentation was sometimes used as an equivalent for the Crucifixion is proved by Stephan Lochner's high-altar for St. Catherine in Cologne (15th c.) where the center panel with the Presentation (now in Darmstadt) took the place of the Crucifixion. (Cf. L. Brandt, *Stephan Lochner's Hochaltar von St. Katharinen zu Köln*. Diss. Hamburg 1938).

The color scheme of the picture is simple. The ground is white. The undergarment of all five figures is red. The cloak of the Virgin is dark blue, while that of St. Joseph and of St. John is yellow. Red is used for the border, red and dark blue for the lunette.

[*Measurements of the square:* 14⅞″ x 11½″]

The customary name for this subject—Holy Family—is not quite adequate from the European point of view, as we have shown in our discussion of the sculptured group (pl. 39). During the Baroque the holy triad—Mary, Joseph and the Child—was often detached from its narrative context and transformed into a devotional image whose meaning was the Holy Trinity on earth. In this painting the trinitarian idea is still further stressed through the appearance of God the Father and the dove of the Holy Ghost over the head of Christ. Read horizontally, the picture represents the terrestrial Trinity, vertically the celestial one.

Apart from its subject matter, this retablo is of special interest as it is based on a composition by Murillo (formerly Munich, Heinemann Gallery), and thus permits us to observe how the the work of a great master has been transformed. In Murillo's painting (cf. fig. 4) the Virgin (on the left) has turned half around towards the Child, while Joseph (on the right) reaches his left arm towards Him. From this arrangement results a spatial movement along curved lines. The New Mexican composition, on the other hand, is static; each parent holds the Child with the hand nearest to Him. In Murillo's painting the folds of the robes are part of a continuous movement, while here the garments of the Virgin and of St. Joseph form a pattern of inverted congruity. Further, most of the colors of one garment reappear on that of the other figure in exchanged positions; thus the red of the lining of Joseph's coat is used for the dress of Mary; the light purple on the outside of his coat is the same as that on the lining of hers. He wears a blue dress (overpainted with green), the color of which we find also on the outside of the Virgin's cloak. The spherical polygon formed in Murillo's composition by the space between the three persons below and God the Father above, has shrunk into a two-dimensional plane in this retablo. Finally, the clouds filled with angels, which Murillo loved so dearly, have been reinterpreted as a black curtain with light incised lines. To sum up, Murillo's spatially conceived composition has been changed into a two-dimensional pattern whose parts are symmetrically arranged, reminiscent of heraldry. Because the process has been complete, without leaving unsolved vestiges, the New Mexican work is in its own way as convincing as its refined prototype.   [*Measurements:* 21 3/4″ x 16″]

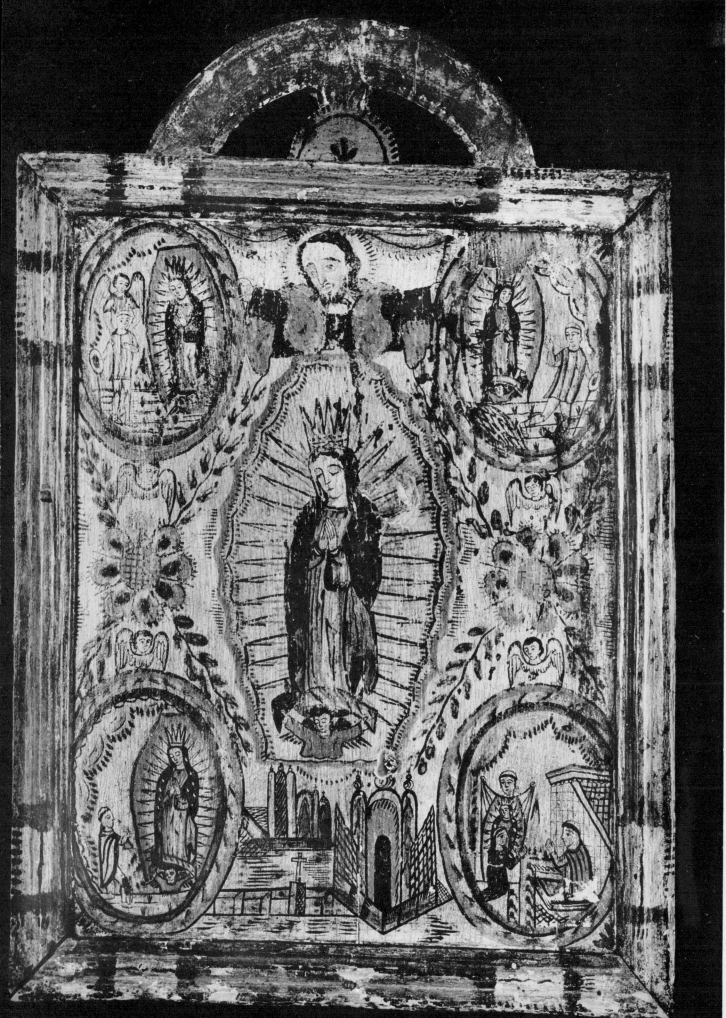

Our Lady of Guadalupe is the most celebrated image of Mexico. The present splendid shrine, successor to humbler structures, was built in 1709 over the spot where in December 1531 the Madonna had appeared to the Indian neophyte, Juan Diego. She ordered him to go before the Bishop of Mexico and to direct him to build a church at the very place where he had seen her. The bishop, who did not believe Juan, asked for a sign. Later, when the Indian met her again, he informed her of the bishop's request, whereupon the Virgin told him to gather roses among the rocks. Although he knew it was neither the place nor the time for roses, he obeyed and found them immediately. After having gathered them in his cloak, he brought them to the bishop. When he unwrapped the cloak, the roses fell out, and on the coarse cloth of the tilma, the picture of the Virgin had miraculously appeared. This picture is the famous relic of Guadalupe (Cf. fig. 2.)

We have told the legend in its more important stages, in order to explain the four scenes in the corners of our retablo. The center is taken up by the image itself. The half figure of God the Father appearing over the head of the Virgin often occurs in the early examples of the Immaculata in Italy as well as in Spain (cf. Tormo, p. 27 seq.). On either side the space is filled with angels and roses, symbolically alluding to the miracle, while in the center below there are two buildings surrounded by a wall, evidently a schematic rendering of the present building.

In the center the Virgin is represented as she appeared to Juan Diego, an erect crowned figure in an attitude of prayer. Her body is surrounded by an aureole whose rays have the form of sharp spikes. She stands on the black crescent of the moon. Both Virgin and moon are supported by an angel, half merged in a cloud. He holds the ends of the Virgin's garment in his upraised arm, like the antique Caelus, personification of the sky, who holds the cosmic cloak over his head.

In iconographic respects the figure of the Virgin is a fairly accurate copy of the original Guadalupe. The differences are mainly of a stylistic nature. While the Guadalupe is given the soft forms of the fully developed Renaissance, our slender, more erect figure has been reduced to its late medieval stage, for folk art like the art of the Middle Ages has a graphic expression. Similarly the aureole is described rather than represented by the spike-shaped beams and its outer circle of flames has been reduced to a mere red zigzag frame. The colors used in the picture are red, blue (in various shades), and black. The frame is painted in such a way as to emphasize the composition.

The history of the type to which the Guadalupe belongs has been discussed on pl. 14. For a legend of a similar type we refer to the celebrated image of Soriano, the true portrait of St. Dominic, which was presented by the Virgin to the Dominicans of Soriano in 1530, the year before she let her likeness miraculously appear on the coat of the poor Mexican Indian. It is quite feasible that the Guadalupe legend was patterned after that of Soriano.

[*Measurements of board:* 19½" x 16"]

A sudarium with the Holy Trinity instead of the features of Christ is extremely rare. As a matter of fact, we are not able to quote any other example of this peculiar subject matter, nor can we tell whether it was a definite religious belief, or merely personal fancy which caused the santero to choose this type. Dr. Erwin Panofsky, who has examined photographs of this specimen, finds the representation clearly heretical, since the sweat cloth of Veronica showed the features of the Incarnate Son, not of the Trinity. Had this occurred in any of the established Catholic centers, it would have constituted an act of heresy, which serves to show how far removed colonial New Mexico was from the rest of the world.

We have pointed out before (pl. 49) that the three-headed Trinity, although forbidden since 1745, was nevertheless greatly cherished in New Mexico. It may well be, therefore, that the retablo was made under its influence. There is further a possibility that the painter intended to produce a Trinity in the first place and that he merely used the iconographic type of the Veronica for this purpose. The figure which we call Veronica may have represented the Virgin to him. It is true, from the iconographical viewpoint, a Trinity and the Virgin in the shape of a Veronica is just as unique as a Veronica with a threefold Deity on her sudarium. However, the latter would be less offensive to the theologians.

The colors of our painting are black and red; some blue is used for the borders. Its graphic style is crude yet quite effective.   [*Measurements:* 19⅜″ x 13¾″]

Close examination of this retablo reveals that the preliminary drawing was not independently done, but rather with the aid of some model. Hence, the weak curves of the arms and the contours of the legs which indicate that some expedient was used. An untrained draughtsman would have transformed the human body into a clumsy abstraction. This drawing, on the other hand, is not awkward but shows the hesitant hand of one who copies with the help of mechanical devices.

Nevertheless, the picture is not without merit. The smooth flow of the contours of the nude parts of the body are the more pleasing since the blue loin cloth causes a sudden interruption. The peculiar form of the loin cloth is reminiscent of certain sculptured representations of the crucified Christ (cf. pl. 50). The conventionalized head attracts the strongest attention in the composition. Here, it seems, the draughtsman is left to his own devices. The uninterrupted outline of brow and nose, the crescent-shaped eyes, and the two black prongs of the beard recall the preciseness of early Spanish illuminated manuscripts.

The entire picture plane around the figure is filled in with black. The two trees with their red leaves and white branches (the white of the gesso undercoat) are pleasant decorative motifs which occur on many retablos of the crucifixion, although their form may vary. The multiple frame consists of areas in red, ocher, and blue.

The retablo offers an interesting iconographic problem. The artist has moved the side wound from the right, where tradition places it, to the side of the heart. The question arises whether he permitted himself this liberty of his own accord.

During the 16th and 17th centuries the minds of the spiritual leaders of the Catholic world were occupied with meditation on the terrestrial life of Christ, as had been the case in the Middle Ages. With respect to the crucifixion of Christ, one discussed ardently whether He was nailed to the cross while it was still on the ground, or after it had been erected; whether three nails were used, or four; whether or not He wore the crown of thorns on the cross; and also, whether the side wound was inflicted on His left or right.

The age in which the sense for historical truthfulness was born and which laid the foundations for future development in the sciences, completely overlooked the fact that for the Middle Ages the side wound had, above all, a symbolic meaning. It had to be on the side which was the "right" one in the heraldic sense, the side where the victorious Ecclesia, personification of the Triumphant Church, was standing, opposite the vanquished Synagogue. For Ecclesia gathered the precious blood which poured out of the side wound into a chalice, profound symbolism of the Holy Communion, of which a vestige can still be found in the cup-bearing angel (cf. pl. 46).

The Baroque was an age in which simple and clear rules were no longer handed out to the artist. It was left to him whether he wanted to follow the new ideas or continue in the tradition. Most of them preferred the traditional type, while a few introduced the innovations which the theologians had suggested.

It is surprising to find our New Mexican santero among the minority. The type which he chose is exceedingly rare in New Mexico. We know of only one other example, which is in the collection of the Hispanic Society in New York (cf. *Ten Panels Probably Executed by the Indians of New Mexico.* 1926). This retablo shows Christ on the cross, in the angles of which there are four winged but bodiless angels, surrounded by a large, common halo. Except for this detail, the resemblance between the two panels is so close that identity of authorship cannot be doubted. Since the same man chose the unusual type twice, we must conclude that it had a special importance to him. Perhaps a faint echo of the controversy among the European theologians had reached his ears.   [*Measurements:* 21½" x 14¼"]